ROAD TO DIGNITY
Socio-Economic Rehabilitation of Valmikis

About the Author

M. Z. Khan (*b.* 1936), MSW Ph.D., F.I.S.C., started his professional career as Assistant Professor at the University of Saugar (1962-79). He briefly served with the Ministry of Welfare (1978-79) and Ministry of Home Affairs (1979-83) before joining Jamia Millia Islamia as Professor of Social Work, a position he continues to hold.

Professor Khan is associated with several governmental, professional and voluntary organisations. He has conducted many studies and successfully implemented several research projects sponsored by national and international agencies. In 1983, he was awarded the prestigious Kumarappa-Reckless Award for his contribution to correctional literature. In 1991, Calcutta University awarded him a medal for his studies on drug dependence. Apart from newspaper articles, he has published about 80 papers in scientific journals in India and abroad. Besides, he has authored twelve books including *Profile of a Nyaya Panchayat, Drug Use amongst College Youth, Work by Jail Inmates, Trends in Family Welfare Planning, Scheduled Caste, and Elderly in Metropolis.*

Archana Dassi took her Masters degree in Social Work in 1991. She started her professional career as Child Counsellor. For a brief period, she was Assistant Project Officer in a community-based project of an NGO. During 1992-1997, she served as Senior Research Assistant with the Department of Social Work, Jamia Millia Islamia and was subsequently appointed Lecturer–a position she continues to hold. Her major research interests include children, their problems, and social deviance–issues on which she has researched and published a number of papers.

ROAD TO DIGNITY

Socio-Economic Rehabilitation of Valmikis

M.Z. KHAN

ARCHANA DASSI

Published for

SULABH INTERNATIONAL SOCIAL SERVICE ORGANISATION, NEW DELHI

by

CONCEPT PUBLISHING COMPANY, NEW DELHI-110 059

ISBN 81-7022-727-5

First Published 1998

Published and Printed by
Ashok Kumar Mittal
Concept Publishing Company
A/15-16, Commercial Block, Mohan Garden,
NEW DELHI - 110059 (India)

Phones : 5649024, 5648039
Fax No. : 91-11-5648053

FOREWORD

It is a matter of serious thought and concern that several population groups in the country remain socially handicapped despite decades of change and development. So-called scavenging castes make for a classic example. Centuries of neglect, deprivation and repression have pushed them into abysmal ignorance, illiteracy and penury. What is more, they have come to accept their peripheral existence as something pre-ordained. This in part explains the indifferent impact of development schemes evolved and implemented to better their lot. In fact, this calls for many things to be done simultaneously.

This is exactly what Sulabh International Social Service Organisation has attempted throughout: Promote low-cost sanitation, wean away scavengers from traditional occupations and rehabilitate them–educationally and occupationally. In this, Sulabh Vocational Training Centres are a vital link.

Although, the vocational training centre at New Delhi has been in existence for quite some time, its organisation and functioning have been systematically appraised by Professor M.Z. Khan and Ms. Archana Dassi for the first time. I am glad to note that not only does the work in hand takes stock of what is being done but also it indicates directions in which this and other centres could be further developed to achieve their avowed goal of putting young persons from socially handicapped families on the path of self-reliance and dignity. Instructors and others would do well to go through it. Besides, the work deserves the attention of all those who have a stake in a balanced and all-round growth and development of the country.

DR. BINDESHWAR PATHAK

FOREWORD

It is a matter of [illegible] that [illegible] a sizeable population group in the country [illegible] downtrodden despite decades of change and development. So-called scavenging castes [illegible] as a class [illegible] of neglect. Humiliation and repression have pushed them into abysmal ignorance, illiteracy and poverty. What is more, they have come to accept their [illegible] existence as something preordained. This is not [illegible] that specific development schemes be evolved and implemented to better their lot. In fact, this calls for many things to be done simultaneously.

This is exactly what the International Sulabh Social Service Organisation has attempted. In [illegible] movement towards sanitation, wean away scavengers from traditional occupation and rehabilitate them economically and occupationally. In this, Sulabh Vocational Training Centres are a vital link.

Although the vocational training centre at New Delhi has been in existence for quite some time, its organisation and functioning have been systematically appraised by Professor M.Z. Khan and Ms Archana Dass for the first time. I am glad to note that not only does the work in hand takes stock of what is being done, but also it indicates directions in which this and other centres could be further developed to achieve their avowed goal of putting young persons from socially handicapped families on the path of self-reliance and dignity. Institutions and individuals would do well to go through it, since the work deserves the attention of all those who have a stake in a balanced and all-round growth and development of the country.

DR. BINDESHWAR PATHAK

ACKNOWLEDGMENTS

NOTIONS of social inequality rise in the minds of men and, therefore, concepts of social equality have to be formed in the minds of men–so as to usher in an equitable and just social order. This is what Sulabh Vocational Training Centre–an innovative and dynamic organisation--aspires for. Studying this organisation and its functioning has been a challenging task that we could not have satisfactorily completed without the unflinching help and cooperation from many quarters.

Dr. Bindeshwar Pathak, Founder of Sulabh Movement and the moving spirit behind the SVTC, has taken the initiative for this work. Not only has he provided necessary support but also he has taken a keen interest at all stages of the work.

Dr. A.K. Lal, A.N. Sinha Institute of Social Studies (he has also been associated with Sulabh Movement from the very beginning), has been all along enthusiastic about the work and has provided much-needed logistic support. The contribution Shri R.N.Verma, Smt. Sheel Prasad, Kumari Anita Jha, Shri Anil Kumar and Shri Raman Kumar to the work has been substantial and significant.

The greatest debt of gratitude is owed to the SVTC trainees and ex-trainees. During information-gathering, they have been understanding and responsive, and have provided much-needed insight. We are equally beholden to the SVTC instructors whose point of view has been a breath of fresh air.

All those named and many who remain unnamed have immensely contributed to what the work has been able to achieve. Their debt is gratefully acknowledged. However, the responsibility of the views expressed and of shortcomings is that of ours alone.

M.Z.KHAN
ARCHANA DASSI

CONTENTS

1

INTRODUCTION

THE INCONGRUITY of an entire population group being relegated not only to the lowest rung of the social ladder but also to such inhuman and degrading work as carrying head-loads of night-soil has been obvious to everyone--for long. To lessen the indignity of the situation, Akbar the Great gave, ages ago, to the members of this caste group, the honorific of *mehtar,* noblest in the community. Did it help? If at all, the meaning of the word underwent a change. Later, much later, Mahatma Gandhi made use of yet another honorific, *harijan,* sons of God. This word, too, almost in no time, turned into some kind of a pejorative. Perhaps much of this intransigence could be traced to caste traditions crystallised over millennia.

India's socio-religious traditions have several distinctive features (Singh, 1973), the foremost among them being social stratification or hierarchical structure. The philosophical relationship between *atma* and *parmatma* as well as the concept of transmigration of soul also contribute to, and reinforce, the inherited and ascriptive *varna* or caste hierarchy. Depending upon their background and perspective, writers have viewed it from several angles. For example, Dumont (1970) regards caste as an ideological system; Furnivall (1939) as cooperating parts of a social whole; and Sherring (1974) as promoting cleanliness and order. Affecting descent, occupation and rituals, the system is an all-encompassing characteristic of Hindu society (Beteille, 1965). Its values and institutions influence all other interpersonal and inter-group relations. Berreman (1979) considers caste-system as a living environment. It represents a multilinear tradition--creating differential groups and subgroups including Valmiki (Hutton, 1955; Joshi 1968).

As is known, the caste system has a bearing on the ownership and control of economic resources as also on occupational opportunities. Until recently, only twice-born or members of the upper caste (Brahmin, Kshatriya and Vaishya) owned primary resources, and those of the lower castes worked for them. Similarly, the former monopolised more prestigious and more remunerative jobs as well as trade and commerce. On the other hand, low-paying work, menial jobs and so-assumed unclean work were passed to or thrusted upon those at the lower social rungs. This is what led to the emergence of such anomalous practices as unapproachability and untouchability (Desai, 1978). Let alone inter-sitting or inter-dining, members of certain Sudra caste groups were prohibited to approach or touch members of upper caste groups as this would pollute and defile them. Doubtless, Valmikis were one of them.

Thus, for centuries, certain population groups have been labelled as untouchable castes. That members of these caste groups, generation after generation, are regarded lowest in caste hierarchy is a small matter. Of course, caste system was and is characterised by a plethora of values, norms and practices governing interaction at personal and group levels. Indeed, these were well-defined and rigidly adhered to, particularly in inter-group relations. What was peculiar to Sudras, especially untouchable castes, were civil disabilities.

Caste norms required Sudras to have segregated housing, mostly at the periphery of the village, sometimes in small hamlets removed by a respectable distance. They could not draw water from community well or pond. Often Sudra women would wait by the village well for hours on end that somebody would graciously pour some water into their vessel also. Of course, they were totally kept away from education including training in martial arts. They could tend cows but they were not supposed to consume cow-milk. Similarly, they were forbidden to ride a horse or palanquin (Dumont, 1970). They could not share seat (cot, platform, etc.) with a twice-born and, during interaction, if necessary, they would squat on the ground at a distance and talk. Ironically enough, these institutionalised disabilities also applied to worship and rituals. They would celebrate Dussehra, Deepawali, Holi, etc. separately, sometimes a day in advance. Of course, their entry in temples was banned. Irony of the situation was that not only were these civil disabilities imposed by members of upper castes but also accepted and acted upon by lower castes. The gut issue however is--Have these anamolous and unjust incongruities diminished?

This kind of labelling presumably enters in the collective psyche of the members of untouchable caste groups. Singly and collectively, they conduct themselves in the community in accordance with these caste norms. Having no right to own immovable property, they had a marginalised existence. They worked for others (members of upper castes) as land tenants, sub-tenants, share-croppers or merely as bonded labour. On the side, some of them would raise goats or pigs and flay dead animals--a few of them would also consume carrion and alcohol. On the top of it, they were assigned so-presumed unclean tasks of assisting child-birth and removing night-soil.

Needless to add, the four quarters of the country have a scavenging caste group with one nomenclature or the other (see Pathak, 1991; Shyamlal, 1992). If in western India, they are known as Bhangi or Ghare, in eastern India they are called Hadi or Mehtar. Likewise, in north India they are known as Bhangi or Mehtar and in south India as Hela. May it be noted that, in contemporary times, there are more than one caste groups which provide this essential service. These include Bhangi, Chuhra and Valmiki (in the present work, the term Valmiki has been used for all of them).

It follows that scavenging used to be more or less a hereditary occupation. If one is born in a scavenger family, he or she when of age had to take up this profession. Seldom was any attention paid to occupational hazards, hygiene or health. On the one hand, society required scavengers to remove night-soil with hands and carry buckets on their hip or head and, on the other, they were socially looked down upon and, even shunned for their unclean work (Pathak, 1991). Taken together, the chore of scavenging was bad enough, the collective attitude towards it made it worse.

It is amazing that we have at our hands an institutionalised arrangement to force unclean work upon a whole section of population and consign them to perpetual social degradation. In contemporary times, scavenging is anomalous and anachronistic. Apparently, it has been the fount from which has flown the practice of unapproachability which Mahatma Gandhi regarded as sin against God (Mohan Rao, 1968).

Changing Socio-political Environment

The twentieth century has been characterised by intellectual, socio-cultural and political liberalisation. Owing to this, even in pre-independence times the problem of depressed classes or exterior castes, especially of Valmikis, attracted much attention. However, the concern with depressed classes seldom went beyond lip-service and, occasionally, political manipulation. Nevertheless, the matter with post-independence period was a little different.

In 1948, the practice of untouchability was abolished by the Untouchability Offences Act which was modified (in the light of Article 17, Constitution of India) and rechristened, in 1955, as the Protection of Civil Rights Act. Articles 341 and 342 enjoin the state to notify these backward sections of population and initiate policies and programmes for their upliftment. Towards this, a constitutional authority, Special Officer for Scheduled Castes and Scheduled Tribes (Article 338) was created which has now been converted into a full-fledged Commission for Scheduled Castes and Scheduled Tribes. In 1995, National Commission on Scavengers was set up to look into the practice of scavenging and living conditions of those engaged in scavenging.

As of now, cash and kind incentives are offered to students belonging to Scheduled Castes, educational institutions have for them seat reservation, government organizations and public sector undertakings have job-reservation, and state and national legislatures have constituencies reserved for them.

The process of planned development has seemingly taken into account the condition of these underdeveloped population groups. Apart from *generic* development programmes, *selective* schemes have also been launched under such programmes as Integrated Rural Development Programme and Jawahar Rozgar Yojana. Under Indira Awas Yojana, in rural areas, they are helped to have proper housing. Likewise, both at the national and state levels, Scheduled Castes Finance and Development Corporations have been set up which offer grants and soft loans to members of Scheduled Castes for self-employment and business.

In this regard, a mention may be made of non-governmental organizations. Quite a few of them have contributed significantly to the improvement of the quality of life of these population groups. These include Harijan Sewak Sangh, Dr. B.R. Ambedkar Research Institute, Ramakrishna Mission, Akhil Bharat Anusuchit Jati Parishad, Servants of India Society, Jana Kalyan Samiti and Shoshun Unmoolan Parishad.

Contemporary Scene

General observation and empirical evidence indicate that, although caste distinctions have gone down, caste feelings have gone up. To this, political processes and media of mass communication have, directly or indirectly, contributed much. On the other hand, during past forty years and more, the upliftment of Scheduled Castes has seldom been in keeping with policy intents and planning goals (Prakash, 1989). Their share in education, services and business does not conform even to their population proportion, what to say of making up the backlog (Masilamani, 1986; Dogra, 1990).

It follows that Valmikis too are tacitly paying the price on account of the slow pace of social and economic change. Their educational and occupational status continues to be low, and their proportion among those below the poverty-line high (Nanduram, 1988).

Socio-economic Problems of Valmikis

It is worth noting that most Sudra castes, particularly Valmikis, since time immemorial, have been leading a sub-human existence (Ram, 1980). Not only have they been socially marginalised but also they themselves have reconciled with social inequities (Thakur, *et al.,* 1984). Towards the curtailment of civil liberties and low standard of living, they have come to have an indifferent, apathetic or even stoic attitude. Apparently, one of their foremost problems is *low self-esteem.*

Valmikis reportedly have umpteen health problems. They have low access to health information and services. Among them mortality rates are high. So is also the matter with birth rate and population growth rate.

During past four decades and more, the network of

Primary Health Centres and Sub-centres (which is supposed to provide health care in rural areas) has hardly been able to bridge the gap.

Literacy and education are the fount from which flow all changes and progress. In sharp contrast, literacy rate among Valmikis is woefully low. In 1981, in India, literacy rate among Scheduled Castes including Valmikis, was only 21 per cent. In 1991, it did move up but only marginally. It was still lower among women (4 per cent). Doubtless, this is a disappointing situation, reservation in educational institutions and incentives, notwithstanding.

Scheduled Castes in general, and Valmikis in particular, continue to take to less prestigious (and sometimes socially degrading) and low-paid work. Their share in agricultural daily-wage work, construction work, sanitation and waste disposal is high and in skilled work and middle and higher levels in government departments public sector undertakings and corporate sector is low (Shah, 1985; Prasad, 1990). Moreover, there has been a dearth of organization or unionization in whatever sector they work which has been a limiting condition in the expansion of facilities and benefits to them.

It follows that most Valmikis are able to raise income hardly sufficient to keep body and soul together (Rao, Bhatt and Venkataraman, 1989). More often than not, several members of a household work and even then many of their basic needs remain unmet. Hardly surprising that their proportion among those below the poverty-line far exceeds their populating proportion.

Their low educational and occupational status leads to palpably low participation in community affairs and politics– reservation in houses of legislature notwithstanding. At mohalla and village levels, their carrying weight or conviction is rather an exception. As a consequence, matters relating to development are decided by others *for* them rather *with* them.

On the other hand, when policy-makers and programme planners think of Valmikis, they think of minimum intervention and perhaps minimum resource inputs (Ram, 1980). Rarely do they have conditions conducive for the fullest exploitation of their talent. As a consequence, grandiloquent educational, skill development, income-generation, health and family welfare and awareness-generation programmes have been pursued, decade after decade, without producing desired results.

At any rate, in any social intervention strategy designed to improve the quality of life of Valmikis, the most critical issue will be work–psychologically satisfying and economically gainful work. It may be added that this kind of approach would be relevant to all groups of Valmikis, whether educationally or skill-wise low or high.

Sulabh Movement

Sulabh movement has roots in *Bhangi Mukti Andolan* which the father of Nation, M.K. Gandhi, initiated in early 30s. It was directed towards liberating Valmikis who had the hereditary occupation of manually removing night-soil from house to house. In the turmoil of freedom struggle, independence and partition of the country, the movement could receive at best a second priority. Nonetheless, the issue remained alive and several schemes were implemented by government and non-governmental organizations making but an indifferent impact.

However, the matter underwent a radical change in 1970: *Sulabh International Social Service Organisation* (formerly Sulabh Shauchalaya Sansthan) was organised by an illustrious Gandhian worker Dr. Bindeshwar Pathak (Pathak, 1991). It aimed at restoring human dignity to Valmikis by liberating them from the demeaning and degrading practice of scavenging, promoting among them modern education and rehabilitating them socially and economically. To translate these revolutionary ideas, Sulabh International Centre for Action Sociology has been set up.

It would be readily seen that Sulabh movement has a down-to-earth approach to the problem of casteism, untouchability and scavenging. It envisages a rhythmic balance between attacking the cause and healing the effect. On the one hand, it articulates dissent on the caste system which perpetuates discrimination and inequities, and advocates giving up of socially and psychologically degrading occupations and, on the other, it envisages conditions and services which provide educational and occupational choices to Valmikis, paving the way for their educational, occupational and social reintegration into the mainstream. This in view, a large number of modern schools and vocational training institutes under the aegis of Sulabh International Centre for Action Sociology have been set up.

The first Sulabh Vocational Training Centre (SVTC) was set up in Patna in 1985. It offered vocational training to young boys and girls (from Valmiki families) in several trades. By all accounts, the SVTC in Patna was quite effective in realising its objectives. Quick on heels, another SVTC, in collaboration with the Government of Maharashtra, was set up in Bombay. It offered to adolescents vocational training programmes in keeping with market demands in Mumbai. Reportedly, it has been quite successful and continues to attract the attention of trainees and employers alike. Yet another SVTC was organised, in 1992, in Delhi. At present it offers training facilities in five trades (two more have been added recently). Although relatively new, it is quite popular. The present work is concerned, in the main, with this training facility.

PRESENT STUDY

The foregoing account brings out that vocational training centres organised under the auspices of Sulabh International Centre for Action Sociology have a history and purpose behind them. In these, considerable amount of thought and resources have been invested. Nonetheless, their critical appraisal is imperative for reasons more than one. There are several issues which have a direct bearing on their functioning and effectiveness. Doubtless, much has been done by way of providing accommodation, equipment and services of trained instructors. The issue however is: Do these resource-inputs measure up to the requirements?

Effectiveness of educational and training institutions directly hinges upon the commitment, background and skills of the educators or instructors. This is more so applicable to an innovative facility like Sulabh Vocational Training Centre which aspires not only to impart vocational skills but also to mitigate a social problem. Doubtless, instructors in these centres have been selected with care and caution. But are they achieving what they are supposed to achieve?

On the other hand, an educational and training institution is as good as its students or trainees. Should they have potential, curiosity and motivation, they would be quick on the uptake and they would learn fast. In the present case, there are however certain limiting conditions: Most of them would hardly fair well on these yardsticks–on account of socio-cultural background they come from. Nonetheless, it would be more than an idle curiosity to ascertain their level of involvement and motivation in programmes they are participating in. Likewise, it seems equally relevant to ascertain the impact of training centres run by Sulabh International Social Service Organisation in terms of (a) economic rehabilitation of those who have undergone training and (b) their social adjustment or readjustment with those they interact in their daily life.

Keeping these issues in view, it is proposed to take a closer look at this innovative programme with the following objectives:

- To look into the organization and functioning of Sulabh Vocational Training Centre in Delhi;
- To examine the background, involvement and enthusiasm of young boys and girls undergoing these training programmes;
- To critically analyse the process of skill development in these trainees; and
- To ascertain the impact of these training programmes in terms of participation of the trainees in productive work as well as their socio-economic reintegration.

Sulabh Vocational Training Centre, New Delhi, attracts a large number of boys and girls, especially from the neighbourhoods situated in the southern parts of the metropolis. The present work focuses on this training centre.

Further, a kind of stock-taking is to be done of existing training facilities. Towards this, instructors, trainees and passed-out trainees are to be contacted. The information thus gathered and analysed is likely to fulfil the objectives of the study.

Location

The Sulabh Vocational Training Centre (SVTC) in New Delhi is located at Mahavir Enclave by the Palam-Dabri Marg. This has fairly acceptable training infrastructure and offers a number of market-relevant trades. Although the facility is primarily meant for boys and girls from Valmiki families, quite a few non-Valmiki young persons also participate in it. It is this training centre which is the focus of the present work.

In order to secure a comprehensive insight into the organization and functioning of the SVTC, persons involved in its management have to be interacted with. For a systematic understanding of a skill-development programme, the viewpoint of trainees, particularly those from Valmiki households, is a critical component. Besides, the situation of those who have passed out from the SVTC and are in the community engaged in work or otherwise has to be looked into. Likewise, it is imperative to ascertain the opinion of those who are employing or supervising such former trainees. Given these considerations, the study has study sample as shown in Figure 1.1.

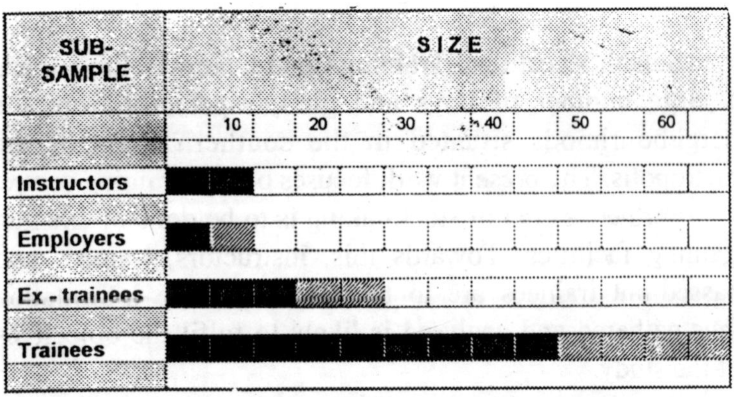

FIG. 1.1: Study sample targeted and completed

This apart, efforts are to be made to interact with those who are involved in the management of the SVTC at higher levels.

Tools and Data Collection

Keeping the objectives of study and sampling design in

mind, two sets of tools have been developed: (a) proformae for the collection of census and official data, and (b) interview schedules for the collection of first-hand data from those included in the study sample. Development and finalisation of interview schedules for instructors, trainees and employers have involved considerable deliberation and effort. These schedules have items dealing with personal background, training infrastructure, training process, market relevance of trades and social dynamics.

Collection of official and primary data has been done concurrently. While instructors and trainees have been contacted at Sulabh Vocational Training Centre, ex-trainees and their employers at their work place. To this process of information gathering, a valuable contribution has been made by Dr. Bindeshwar Pathak, founder of Sulabh International Social Service Organisation.

Analysis and Report

The information thus gathered from these diverse sources has been analysed in quantitative and qualitative terms. Using simple statistical techniques and graphic presentation, the information has been presented in a manner that maximises the realization of the study objectives.

All this information, analyses and interpretation have been organised in the form of a report which, put together, sheds light on the road to dignity which is paved by challenges and opportunities as far as Valmiki boys and girls are concerned. The report has six sections: Introduction, Support Structures, Potentials and Capabilities, Capacity Building, Programme Outcomes and Conclusion.

Taken together, the report is likely to shed light on the viability of the SVTC-thrust, namely, the socio-economic reintegration of a socially disadvantaged population group into the mainstream of national life.

2

SUPPORT STRUCTURES

AT THE OUTSET, a reference may well be made to the Sulabh Movement. As is well known, it was launched by Dr. Bindeshwar Pathak, in 1970. For this, he drew inspiration from *Bhangi Mukti Andolan* which the Father of the Nation, M.K. Gandhi, had initiated in early thirties. Indeed, Sulabh Movement was very much in keeping with the ideals and aspirations of an egalitarian and modern nation.

On the other hand, Sulabh Movement markedly differed from earlier ideas and movements concerning scavengers. A dispassionate look would readily show that this movement went beyond *intention* and spawned *action* which was as much in the interest of Valmikis as of the people and the country. Visionary and action-oriented, the movement took a holistic view of the problems confronting this underprivileged population group with a view to initiating programmes having the ability to bring about a positive and sustained change in their social situation.

Age-old traditions compelled and impelled Valmikis to lead a marginalised existence. This was evident from the way they performed their daily life activities, dressed, ate, drank and so on. Some of their practices were indeed loathsome and some were used by others as a pretext for distancing them. Workers in Sulabh Movement were aware of these realities; but they also realised that these problems were hardly amenable to direct intervention.

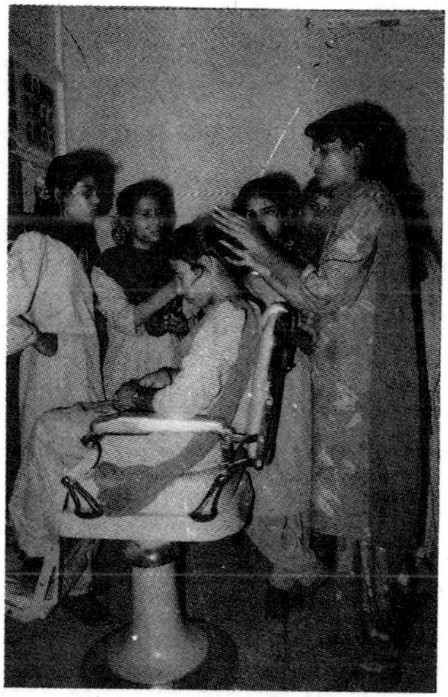

Valmikis did have a range of critical needs, yet most of them were hardly conscious of them. In the main, these included literacy and education, self-esteem and social inter-mixing. On the one hand, caste norms and practices operated invariably to their disadvantage and, on the other, they themselves were unmindful of this. If they rated low in social status on these counts, they tended to reconcile with the situation, perhaps attributing it to their *karma* of their previous births. This problem figured on the top of the agenda of the Sulabh Movement. It organised educational institutions, albeit on a limited scale, and vocational training centres. To enlarge and deepen social interaction it started organising ceremonies and functions in which people from different walks of life would participate by hundreds.

Sulabh Movement was acutely conscious of the hereditary and degrading occupation of the Valmikis–removing night-soil from house to house and sometimes carrying basket or bucket loads on their hip or head. Of course, the practice warranted a frontal attack and, indeed, Sulabh Movement did so. It planned and implemented a low-cost sanitation programme (Pathak, 1981). The idea spread like wild fire and, within two decades, it spanned the entire country. This replaced dry-latrines with inexpensive water closets. This was a boon both for urban slums and remote villages. Among others, this dispensed with the necessity of having workers for handling scavenging work. Was it not a down-to-earth pragmatic approach to hoary traditions and age-old problems?

As of now Sulabh International has grown into a mega organization, manned by more than 35,000 workers. Over the years, it has put up 686,000 low-cost latrines and has built and is maintaining more than 2,000 community toilet complexes. Likewise, 61 biogas-based power-generation plants, based on a highly eco-friendly technology, are on stream in different parts of the country. As a result, more than 37,000 Valmikis have been able to cut away from their hereditary occupation and moved to non-stigmatizing and better-paid work. It would be seen that Sulabh Movement has been a veritable boon to Valmikis–not only in its profession but also in practice. Also, it has benefited people in general. In many cities, towns and villages, people have an alternative to open-air defecation. In public toilet complexes run by Sulabh International Social Service Organization, they have to themselves dignified and hygienic facilities including for washing.

It is this backdrop that makes Sulabh Vocational Training Centre (SVTC) an important milestone in our efforts to put up-and-coming generation from disadvantaged sections on the path leading to self-respect and self-reliance. To what extent is SVTC cut out to fulfil this role?

Sulabh Vocational Training Centre

Looked at from a larger perspective, skill development is an extension of the educational process. It prepares a person not only for a specific job but also for life. Having acquired meaningful and relevant skills, the person is better positioned to engage in productive activities (Papola and Ashraf, 1983). In the process, he moves towards self-reliance and adds to his self-esteem. Also, this elevates, in varying degrees, his status in the family and neighbourhood. Given perseverance and opportunity, he is able to exploit his talents and potential and, more often than not, to prosper. In fact, in the present environment denoted by openness and liberalization, rags-to-riches stories of skilled persons abound through the length and breadth of the country. Doubtless, these persons are moving up on economic and social ladder–and also contributing to the development of the country.

Should Valmiki boys and girls with varying educational background turn to skill-development in market-relevant trades, they are likely to be rewarded in ways more than one. And this is what fully justifies the approach and strategy of Sulabh Vocational Training Centre (SVTC).

Organizational Framework

Indeed, the arrangement of work-relations in the SVTC is simple, informal and purposive. It has to be so–its creation is more a consequence of a passion to rehabilitate Valmiki youngsters and less of any formal sanction or grant. Along with the popularisation of low-cost sanitation, Sulabh International Social Service Organization and its wing, Sulabh International Centre for Action Sociology have paid duc attention to wean Valmikis from scavenging. Aptly it has paid attention to the upcoming generation. SVTC is the main modality in this direction. Nonetheless, it remains largely a small and informal organization.

The SVTC has an Executive Committee (see Figure 2.1). It is a small (membership, 10) and compact policy-making body, having honorary Chairman, Vice-chairman-cum-Director, Treasurer and Secretary. Day-to-day decision-making and overseeing the SVTC functioning are the responsibilities of the Vice-Chairman-cum-Director.

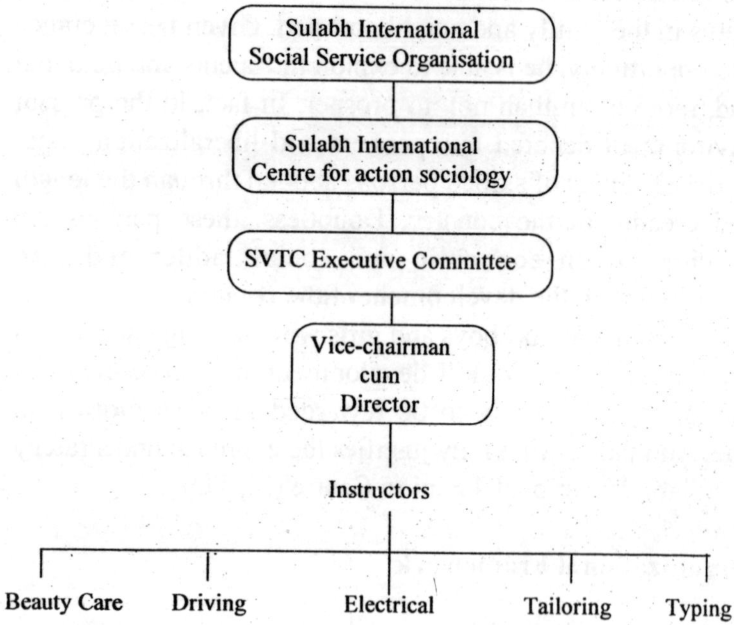

FIG. 2.1: Organisational set-up of the SVTC

As mentioned earlier, the SVTC has five vocational trades (recently three more have been added), details of which are reflected in Table 2.1.

Each trade has an honorary instructor, except Beauty-care and Electrical which have two instructors each. By way of support staff it has some accounts, secretarial and sundry services on sharing basis. Although the SVTC organizational structure is relatively small, it facilitates the fulfilment of its objectives.

TABLE 2.1: Vocational Trades offered by the SVTC

	Duration (months)	Instructors (number)	In-take (trainees)
Beauty-care	6	2	20
Driving	3	1	20
Electrical	6	2	30
Tailoring	6	1	30
Typing	6	1	30

Source: SVTC records.

Financial Structure

It follows that financial arrangements of the SVTC are somewhat informal. It has only one funding source, namely Sulabh International Social Service Organization. Thus far no voluntary, public or international agency has joined hands in this venture, except on one occasion when Ministry of Human Resources Development, GOI, had provided some funds for workshop equipment. Beginning 1995, the practice of charging a token fee of Rs.100 a month has been introduced. However, Valmiki trainees are exempt from the payment of fees. Incidentally , a few Valmiki trainees do not take it in good light. They feel that this differentiation is counter-productive which, among other things, perpetuates caste-differentiation and feelings. Reportedly, budget is regularly formulated and approved by the SISSO (see Table 2.2). It would be seen that budgetary allocations have been

TABLE 2.2: SVTC budget during 1992-95

(In rupees)

Head	1992-93	1993-94	1994-95
Honorarium			
(a) Professional staff	1,21,200	1,21,200	1,37,400
(b) Office staff	28,800	28,80C	52,800
Miscellaneous	57,000	68,800	1,27,200
Total	2,07,000	2,18,800	3,17,400

Source: SVTC records.

TABLE 2.3: Expenditure pattern of the SVTC

(In rupees)

Budget head	1992	1993	1994
Honorarium	32,000	46,000	1,18,600
Stipend	-	-	1,66,205
Training material	5,963	24,606	35,156
Equipment maint.	20,190	49,575	71,318
Local travel	-	3,600	4,200
Miscellaneous	3,874	2,123	15,710
Total	62,027	1,75,904	4,11,189

Source: SVTC records.

steadily increasing.

A glance at Table 2.3 would bring out the expenditure pattern of SVTC during 1992-94. From a little more than Rs. 62,000 the expenditure has risen to Rs. 4,11,189--in just three years. At any rate, the year 1994 had the major expenditure under the budget head 'Stipend' which was paid to trainees neither in the preceding years nor in succeeding years. Leaving aside stipend, more than 48 per cent of the expenditure, in 1994, was on the payment of salaries to staff. Further, a comparison between Tables 2.2 and 2.3 would show that expenditure of the SVTC has been lower than budgetary allocations, except in 1994, the year during which trainees were given stipend.

A look may be had at different functional wings. During 1994, total expenditure on Driving trade was Rs. 91,113, on Electrical trade Rs. 58,366, Tailoring trade Rs. 49,673, and on Typing trade Rs. 41,631 (Beauty-care was introduced only in 1995). Expenditure on salary was highest in Electrical trade (it has two instructors); on training material again in Electrical trade: on maintenance in Driving trade; and on miscellaneous items in Tailoring trade (see Figure 2.2).

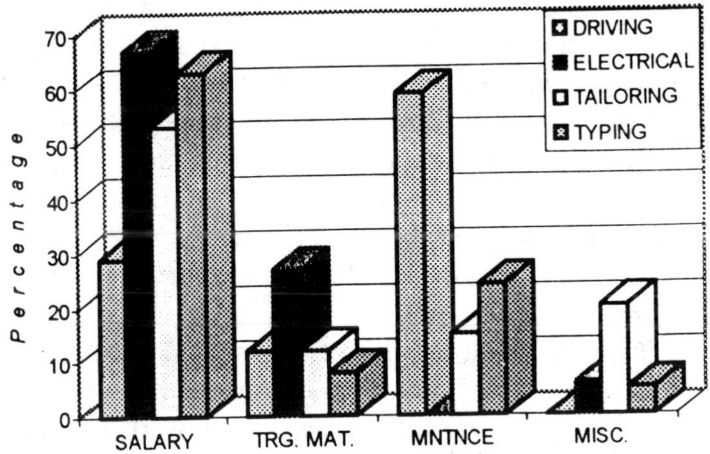

FIG. 2.2: Expenditure Pattern in 1994

Physical Facilities

It is well-established that physical environment has a direct bearing on the motivation of individuals and groups. In educational and training institutions, physical facilities profoundly influence the quality and effectiveness of the intended activities. The significance of these goes up manifold in relation to a vocational training centre. Often acquisition of skill is directly proportionate to such physical facilities as accommodation, equipment and other materials. What is the position of Sulabh Vocational Training Centre?

Located close to the headquarters of Sulabh International Social Service Organization on Palam-Dabri Marg, in New Delhi, Sulabh Vocational Training Centre has its own expansive campus. Simple but elegant plaster-concrete rooms, hum with activities six days a week. In fact, it is an adjunct of Sulabh Public School, which has 15 rooms fitted into a hollow square. Out of these five rooms house SVTC.

In the SVTC, each trade is assigned a room. The size of the room varies with the trade. For example, rooms for Beauty-care and Driving trades are small (12-14 square metres) and for Electrical, Tailoring and Typing trades large (40 square metres). It is ascertained that the size of these rooms have the approval of the local ITI. Likewise, these rooms are outfitted according to the requirements of the trade. To illustrate, the room for Beauty Care Training has mirrors and stuffed revolving chairs, for Electrical trade circuit-boards and work-benches, and for Typing trade tables and chairs. Is this kind of accommodation functional and efficient?

Towards this the opinion of trainees and instructors has been ascertained. Almost all the trainees, former trainees and instructors report that they face in their work no problem in respect of accommodation. However, there are two trainees and three instructors (out of seven) who feel that the space available for Beauty-care and Electrical trade is somewhat insufficient. During working hours the room for Beauty-care trade is found to be relatively crowded.

As would be expected, SVTC has necessary equipment– of course, configuration varies with trade. The Beauty-care trade has mirrors (numbering four), stuffed chair (1), scissors, clippers, pluckers, hair drier, etc. Driving trade has not much inside the room, except for a few tools and auto- and road-sign charts, mounted on wooden boards and fixed on the walls; but outside the room there is a Maruti van used for driving lessons. Electrical trade has ampere-meters, multi-meters, volt-meters, soldering irons, etc. tailoring trade has 21 pedestal sewing machines (none of them are electric-powered) and such paraphernalia as tailoring scale, scissors, chalk, needles, etc. Typing trade has eight typing machines with English keyboard and an equal number with Hindi keyboard. Do we have in SVTC needed equipment?

Again, almost all trainees, former trainees and instructors are satisfied with the range of equipment the SVTC has. Some time back, Ministry of Human Resources Development, GOI, had provided a sum of Rs. 90,000 for the purchase of tools and equipment. Indeed, this has been of great help. However, quite a few of them think that it would do with some more equipment. For example, in Driving trade the range of vehicles could be enlarged to include such vehicles as Ambassador and Padmini cars, auto rickshaw and passenger bus. In Electrical trade, there is reportedly an unending crib over screw-drivers and pliers. Regarding Tailoring trade, suggestions are recurrent for adding electric-powered machines and pekoe and embroidery machines. Concerning Typing trade, quite a few think that some worn out typing machines better be replaced. Besides, new equipment could be added for electronic typing and computer typing.

It goes without saying that in imparting skill-development instructions an amount of consumable material is required. Of course, this requirement varies from trade to trade. For instance, at the SVTC, motor-vehicle driving hardly requires any material other than petrol, and, in contrast, Beauty-care trade requires a wide range of material, that is, cosmetics (quite a few cosmetic items could be very expensive). At any rate, for carrying on instructional programme properly, all the other trades require material: Typing trade: typing paper, Electrical trade: soldering rod and flexible wire; and tailoring: brown paper, needles, bobbin case, tailor's chalk, cloth and thread. May it be noted that while SVTC does provide some of these items, others are to be brought by the trainees themselves. What is the situation at the floor level?

In the opinion of trainees, former trainees and instructors, there is no shortage of required material. However, in some trades a few trainees felt that some more materials could be added to make the programme more smooth and effective. For example, in Typing trade the suggestion was recurrent for typing paper, in Tailoring for brown paper, thread and cloth, and in Beauty-care for wax, bleaching cream and face creams. Among others, this reflects over-dependence on the part of the trainees.

Instructional Facilities

Before proceeding further, a closer look may be had at the background of instructors in SVTC. Beauty-care and Electrical trades have two instructors each, and the rest have one instructor each. Out of the seven instructors three are women (two in Beauty-care and one in Tailoring). Instructors' age ranges from 18 to 60 years (average, 28 years). So does their educational background, from tenth standard to graduation. However, most of them have undergone trade certificate or diploma courses. The emoluments they receive from SVTC vary from Rs. 1400 to Rs. 2200 a month. In fact, three of them work outside to raise additional income and one receives pension. Yet another factor that has a bearing on their functioning is the distance between their residence and SVTC. It ranges between 1 to 15 kilometres (average, 7 kilometres).

Nonetheless, they are generally punctual in attending their duties. On the other side, five of the instructors are Hindu, one Christian and one Sikh. Five of them have Hindi (including two who are comfortable in Bhojpuri dialect) and two have Punjabi as their mother tongue. Out of five instructors professing Hindu religion, only one is from a scheduled caste (a Valmiki, to be precise) and the rest from other castes. Among others, this shows a relative dearth of technically qualified persons among scheduled castes.

The above account brings out that instructors have the requisite qualification and experience to impart skills to trainees in different trades. What is the perception of the trainees? Except one, all the trainees and ex-trainees report that their instructors are competent. The lone dissenter is from Typing trade: The trainee feels that the instructors

could take a little more interest in their work, pay individual attention to trainees and enthuse young minds.

Stipend

To a layman, it would sound rather amusing that beneficiaries of a vocational training programme get stipend. However, it would not remain so amusing, should one pay attention to the targeted population. Coming mostly from lower socio-economic strata of society, Valmiki youngsters often require additional motivation or incentive. Moreover, quite a few of them work to supplement family income; and when they are undergoing a training programme, they and their family suffer wage-loss. Among others, this also shows up in the rates of absenteeism and drop-out. To a great extent, provision of stipend circumvents these stumbling blocks.

At any rate, over the preceding decades, several public vocational training schemes have had provision for stipend. Example may be cited of Training Rural Youth For Self Employment (TRYSEM). Nearly all the trainees participating in TRYSEM are given stipend, amount varying from state to state and, sometimes from programme to programme. May it be noted that this type of incentive has had a critical role in skill development programme implemented in tribal areas.

TABLE 2.4: Stipend Paid to Trainees in 1994

Trade	Amount (in rupees)
Beauty care	–
Driving	76,500
Electrical	17,125
Tailoring	61,380
Typing	11,200
Total	1,66,205

Source: SVTC records.

Nonetheless, there is a subtle difference between the programme sponsored by public authorities and those offered by SVTC. The latter does not receive any public grant, it is funded solely by Sulabh International Social Service Organisation. However, during 1994, trainees in four trades (the fifth Beauty-care was not there, till then) were provided stipend. Each trainee was given Rs. 5000 on the successful completion of the programme. Details of the total expenditure are reflected by Table 2.4.

Note that not all the trainees were paid stipend in cash. For example, those in Electrical trade were provided a tool-kit costing about Rs. 1100, and those in Tailoring a sewing machine costing about Rs. 2100. The balance was in down cash. SVTC authorities state that the amount of Rs. 500 a month to each trainee was less by way of stipend and more a method of providing support to passing out trainees during the period they look for job or work.

It follows that the scheme of stipend or financial support to trainees in the SVTC is not in operation at present. But many youngsters have enrolled themselves with the SVTC under the impression and with hope that at the end of the programme they would receive, as in the preceding year, some cash incentive. One of the instructors connects up the provision of stipend with the problem of absenteeism and drop-out rate, particularly among Valmiki students: Many of them are getting increasingly indifferent or even disenchanted.

Training Contents

It goes without saying that relevance and spread of a skill development programme has something directly to do with the involvement and uptake of the trainees. In this regard SVTC has wholly relied on the instructional format of Industrial Training Institutes (a chain of training centres run by public authorities). In fact, one of the instructors is also an old ITI hand.

This apart, it would be relevant to briefly outline training content of different trades offered by the SVTC.

The syllabi in different vocational trades offered by the SVTC are, indeed, evolving. These are being updated and streamlined year after year in the light of market conditions. However, both instructors and trainees have highly workable syllabi:

(a) *Beauty-care*–Hair dressing: Scalp massage. Bleaching. Waving and straightening. Roller setting. Manicure and pedicure. Facials and make-up.

(b) *Driving trade*–This trade does not have a structured syllabus. However, trainees are familiarised with main parts of motor-vehicle and their function and traffic road-signs. Following this, they are given driving lessons (they are expected to have driving learner's licence with them) by an instructor.

(c) *Electrical trade*–Syllabus for this trade is spread over six months. It includes: familiarization with electrical signs and symbols. Safety. Hand tools and accessories. Measurement tools. Circuits. Types of electrical wires. Cable skinning, joining and soldering. Switches, sockets and holders. Voltage and ampere. Conductors and resistance. Fitting of accessories and appliances. Distribution circuits. Florescent tube. Overhead systems.

(d) *Tailoring*–Needles and threads. Sewing-machine: main parts and maintenance. Dress material: pressing and trimming. Basic stitches: Hemming, smoking, etc. Button and hole. Baby suit, petticoat, and bloomer set. Kurta pyjama. Boy's shirt. Nighty.

(e) *Typing (English and Hindi)*–Main principles. Typewriter: Main parts and maintenance. Touch system. Key board: alpha-numeric and symbol characters. formatting of text. Corrections.

Typing of tables, petitions and contracts. Typing speed and accuracy.

It must be mentioned that, for evaluation or examination, ITI instructors are invited on the completion of training programmes Subsequently, trainees also receive ITI certificates.

SVTC-Trainee Relationship

SVTC aspires, and it ought to aspire, to be more than a training centre. This implies that the trainees identify themselves and feel attached to the organization. Does it happen? Among others, this kind of feeling would be reflected by visits of those who have passed out.

It may be pointed out that the SVTC has come into being relatively recently. As a consequence, the number of alumni is not very large. It is ascertained that two-thirds of the ex-trainees have passed out only 18 months ago and the remaining only a few months ago. Nevertheless, it is heartening to note that all of them, reportedly, keep visiting the centre in Mahavir Enclave. This is also supported by the view of the instructors Interestingly, a fourth of the ex-trainees report that they visit SVTC almost everyday and a half every month.

It would be insightful to look into the reasons for such visits. A large number of trainees call on their *guru* (instructor). They drop in to seek help or guidance on their work-related problems or information on advanced courses. Some of them, especially in Typing trade show up to improve their speed and accuracy in typing. On the other hand, others visit the Sulabh Complex for mundane reasons. They visit daily because they work there (most of them are typists). A few others turn up to collect the arrear amount of their incentive money or certificate (which often takes time as certificates are prepared by ITI). This aside, Sulabh International Social Service Organization organises ceremonies and functions (3 to 4 every year); and ex-trainees are invariably among the invitees to these functions.

To recapitulate, SVTC has a mission and function. It aims to put Valmiki boys and girls on the path of self-respect and to equip them for a meaningful and productive life. Towards this, it has evolved a befitting infrastructure. Relatively new, it is yet to stabilise. Yet it has physical environment, facilities and training inputs which greatly facilitate the realization of its objectives. Maybe, in the years to come, the infrastructure develops further to fulfil its mission and vision much more comprehensively.

3

POTENTIALS AND CAPABILITIES

THERE is no denying the fact that a training institution is as good as its trainees. If trainees are able to pick up new skills or hone the ones they already possess and, on passing out, put them to use in real life-situations, they add to their status as well as to the stature of the institution. This is what explains the value which Sulabh Vocational Training Centre attaches to its trainees. Beyond vocational training routine, trainees are dealt with empathy. Down the line, all Sulabh functionaries treat them as family members. They are almost automatically invited to all Sulabh functions and ceremonies. Further, they are involved in the organizational work of these functions. Many trainees work long and hard to prepare 'cultural' items to be presented during these functions. Besides, in the post-training period, SVTC helps trainees in having gainful placement–may it be a job or self-employment.

Furthermore, SVTC has kept its doors open to non-Valmikis. As Fig. 3.1 would show that, in the five vocational trades, 43 per cent of the trainees are Valmikis, 12 per cent belong to other scheduled castes, and the remaining 45 per cent belong to upper castes or other religious groups. May it be noted that admission procedures of SVTC give priority to Valmiki candidates. Should such candidates be unavailable, the seats are given to candidates from other caste-groups.

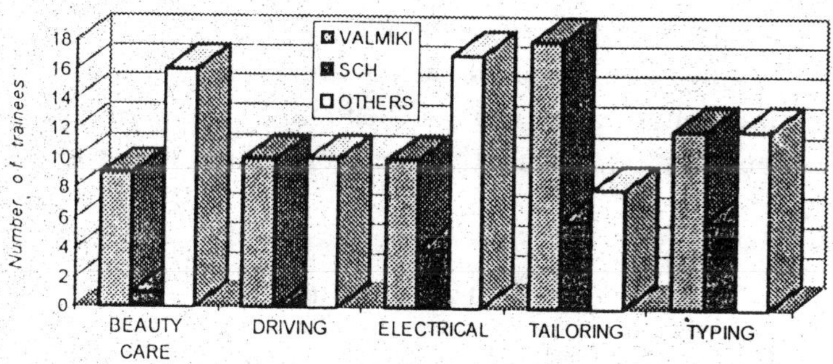

FIG. 3.1 : Caste-composition of trainees

Figure 3.1 would further show that Tailoring has the largest proportion of the Valmiki trainees (56 per cent), and followed by Driving trade (50 per cent). Furthermore, Electrical trade has the smallest proportion of Valmiki trainees that is, 33 per cent (also it has matriculation as minimum educational requirement). Anyway, keeping the trainee group heterogeneous is not without merit: Cost-effectiveness of training programmes tends to go up. Furthermore, process of social inter-mixing is likely to narrow down caste cleavages, howsoever small in scale. By seating Arjunas and Eklavyas side by side, the eventuality of thumb-chopping is likely to be obviated.

This feature of the SVTC is also taken note of by trainees. "I like Sulabh," quipped a girl-trainee, "because Sulabh does not discriminate people on the basis of religion or caste." In sharp contrast, a few Valmiki trainees feel uncomfortable when they are referred to as Valmikis, especially in the presence of outside visitors.

At any rate, the success of a training programme hinges upon the goal-orientation and motivation-level of the trainees. Should they be hospitable to new ideas and keep on picking up new skills, they would learn much more than they are taught. Has the SVTC been able to find and foregather such young persons? Has it adopted any modalities to further raise the motivation of its trainees?

It might be added that in a training situation, motivation, purposiveness and learning depend much on the background of the trainees. This is what the present section is addressed to.

SVTC TRAINEES

It may be reiterated that SVTCs have been in existence for quite some time. Their importance increased when the process of economic liberalization was set in motion, in 1991. This laid an added emphasis on skill-development and self-employment particularly among the less educated. The SVTC started functioning at New Delhi in the year 1992–with barely 36 trainees. This enrollment increased to 91 in 1993, and to 106 in 1994. In 1995, a fifth trade, Beauty care, was introduced which has also added to the trainee-strength, raising it to 139 (by the end of the year the total number of trainees is expected to be much larger). This upward swing in the number of trainees does make for a happy trend. How does SVTC select its trainees?

Admission Procedure

Training programmes offered by the SVTC have prescribed educational qualifications for admission:

Beauty care	10th standard
Driving	10th standard
Electrical	8th standard
Tailoring	10th standard
Typing	10th standard

The procedures adopted for admission to different trades in the SVTC are direct, simple and flexible. It is admission-interview by a committee comprising three functionaries: Vice-chairman-cum-Director, Head Mistress and instructor of the trade concerned. The committee screens all the admission applications and interviews them one at a time. It looks into the social and educational background of the candidates as well as their temperament and occupational preferences. That the committee does not insist on any rigorous and objective methods of evaluation or the administration of aptitude test is understandable: Not only has SVTC to do skill development but also it has a social purpose to fulfil. Thus far, this admission procedure seems to very well fit into the SVTC-scheme.

Trainees: Family Background

Family is the first school of human civilization. Within the matrix of family structure, social norms, values and practices are transferred from one generation to another. Overtly or covertly, a person carries the impress of family ethos. This seems to be particularly important in the present context.

As mentioned earlier, a fifth of the trainees are married. There are four trainees whose father is not alive. Thus, seven trainees out of every ten are living with their natural family. Should attention be paid to these 35 households, father of 10 trainees and mother of 9 trainees are engaged in traditional occupation, namely sanitation work. All others are engaged in private or government service and doing a diverse range of jobs. It is notable that none of the husband of trainees (number, 6) is doing traditional job. Thus a strong trend is discerned about Valmikis shifting for good from their traditional occupation.

At any rate, in most households more than one member is engaged in paid work. Perhaps this is necessary in a metropolitan area to make both ends meet. The household income ranges from as low as Rs. 1100 a month to Rs. 6000. A half of them have a monthly income of Rs. 2500 or above. On the average, the household income is found to be Rs. 2451. These households seem to be relatively and reasonably well off.

Trainees: Personal Background

Improvement of knowledge, modification of attitudes and development of new skills depend much on one's background. SVTC would achieve its purposes to the extent the background of the trainees facilitates it. It is, therefore, imperative that the antecedents of the young boys and girls undergoing training are brought under the focus.

Interestingly enough, at the SVTC there are vocational trades which almost exclusively attract either males or females. To illustrate, Driving trade (total strength, 20; and Valmikis, 9) and Electrical trade (31 and 3) are male-preserves. On the other hand, Beauty Care (26 and 6) and Tailoring (32 and 19) are female domains. Typing trade is the lone exception which has both male (16 and 3) and female (14 and 6) trainees. The trend appears to be consistent when attention is paid to those who have passed out: all ex-trainees in Electrical trade are males and all Tailoring ex-trainees are females: and in Typing all are females except for one ex-trainee. Perhaps this kind of gender-differentiation in vocational trades is culture-determined.

Reportedly, age at marriage among scheduled castes is low (Showeb, 1986). Stated differently, both boys and girls enter into wedlock early in age. Among the trainees the position is rather unclear, as only four of the male trainees and six female trainees are married. That early marriages continue to be solemnised among scheduled castes, comes to the fore when age-distribution among trainees is examined.

As would be expected, most trainees are young in age–age range, 15 to 27 years (see Figure 3.2). Most girls are younger (average age, 18.6 years) than boys (21.8 years). In any case, most trainees are below 20 (overall average age, 19.8 years). So is the case with ex-trainees–their average age is found to be 19.6 years.

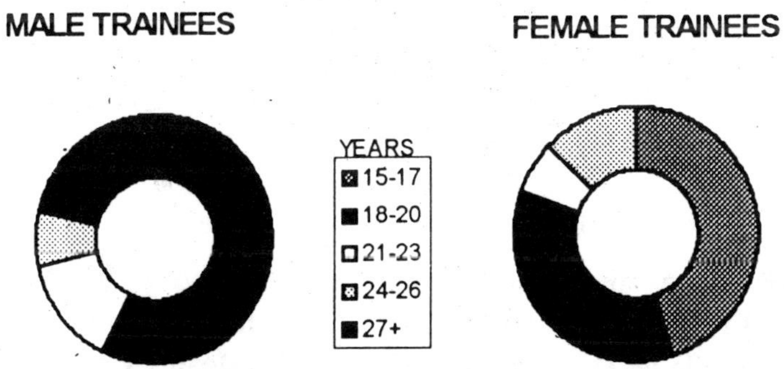

FIG. 3.2: Distribution of age of trainees

It could hardly be gainsaid that education is a prime indicator of one's potential to acquire new skills. On the other hand, most scheduled castes have lagged behind the national average in literacy and education (Showeb, 1986; Aggarwal and Sibou, 1992). What is the position at the SVTC? The set of trainees that it has is rather well off. All the trainees have done some schooling and a few have been to college also (see Figure 3.3). Twenty-seven per cent have done primary education and 4 per cent are graduates (eight trainees are pursuing higher education, side by side). As would be expected, in terms of education girls rate lower than boys.

Besides, there are inter-trade educational differences–for understandable reasons. In Typing trade all the trainees are

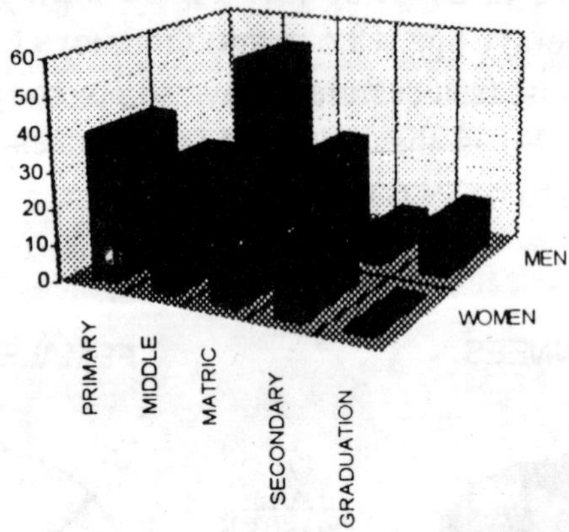

FIG. 3.3 : Educational status of trainees

matriculates and higher. In contrast, in Driving, Electrical and Tailoring trades most of them have done schooling upto the middle level. In the newly introduced Beauty Care trade, distribution of education is somewhat homogeneous. A third of the trainees have done schooling upto primary level, an equal proportion upto middle level, and the remaining have passed their matriculation or senior secondary examination. Taken together, the educational standard of the trainees augurs well for the SVTC programmes.

Interestingly enough, SVTC programme-managers expect bi-lingualism, English and Hindi, from trainees. The same is the story with instructors: Most of them are given to switching from Hindi to English and *vice versa.* In contrast, ground realities are a shade different. There are some trainees who are comfortable both with English and Hindi but there are many more who are only in Hindi. Switching to English during conversation or instruction puts them into an awkward situation. To a great deal, the matter of medium of conversation and instruction seems to cause avoidable confusion.

Although the trainees are in the formative years of their

life, quite a few of them (31 per cent) are doing one paid job or another. One young trainee, in Driving trade is working with a private cargo-contractor. Remaining are self-employed, doing such assorted jobs as car-washing, electric-wiring, stitching and helping people in getting driving licence from State Transport Authority. It is gratifying to note that this occupational pattern, though limited, is quite diversified, and none of the trainees is engaged in 'traditional' trades.

Of course, trainees are able to make some money on the side. One of the trainees, an electrician, makes around Rs. 3000 a month, and some trainees in Tailoring make only Rs. 25 a month. On the average, these trainees earn Rs. 851 a month. Maybe non-working trainees (69 per cent) are also encouraged to take up similar paid work on the side, for it would be good for their self-esteem as well as for their motivation.

SVTC-RESIDENCE DISTANCE

It is not too difficult to make out that the houses, where the trainees live in, are modest in terms of location, area and construction. What is however relevant is their location and the distance from Mahavir Enclave. This dimension assumes importance in the light of general observation that people from weaker sections of population are disinclined to travel long distances–be it for education, training or work. In any case, shorter distances and duration of travel-time are certainly conducive for punctuality, regularity and continuance. Further, this assures physical and mental alertness of the trainees during instruction.

On the other hand, transport system in Delhi is patently rudimentary and unpredictable. Unlike several other metros in the country, the capital city does not have any Rapid Transit System. Denizens of Delhi have to make do with Delhi Transport Corporation and private buses. These buses seldom follow any time schedule and are most of the time overcrowded. This in view, the situation of the SVTC trainees is not too difficult to imagine.

It is however seen that eight trainees out of every ten come from either Mahavir Enclave or adjoining neighbourhoods (Palam Village, Palam Colony, Palam Vihar, Manglapuri, etc.). A few also come from such distant places such as Munirka, Paschim Puri, Uttam Nagar and the like.

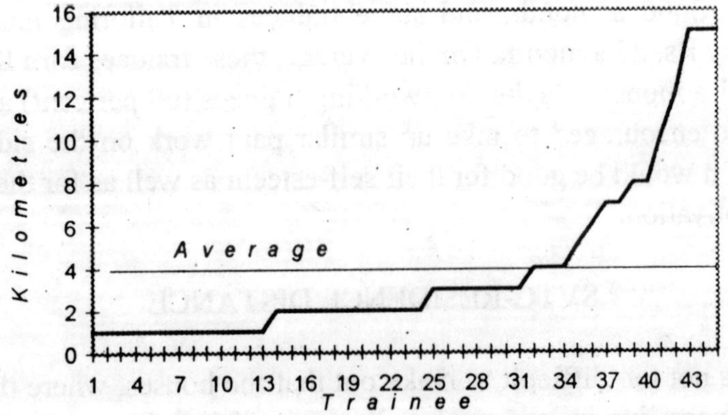

FIG. 3.4: SVTC-Residence distance

Distance between the place of residence and place of work is important everywhere and perhaps crucial in the present context. In respect of youngsters from Valmiki families, reportedly, motivational level is often indifferent. This is aggravated, should educational or training facilities entail long and arduous journey. What is the position in the present context?

It is encouraging to note that 29 per cent of the trainees live within a distance of two kilometres and another 40 per cent within 4 kilometres (see Fig. 3.4). But the remaining 31 per cent commute long distances. Their plight needs to be seen in the context of grossly underdeveloped transport system in Delhi. Reportedly some of the trainees change three DTC buses, spending sometimes more than 90 minutes to reach SVTC.

To sum up, for several historical-cultural reasons, Valmikis have lagged behind in education and development. Not only were they socially deprived but also they themselves were reconciled with their plight and relegated themselves to fate. Given this, enlisting their participation and involving them in such an ambitious enterprise as vocational training is an uphill task. It calls for the convergence of a myriad of favourable conditions.

Nonetheless, it is encouraging to note that the family background and personal factors of the trainees in the SVTC do have variations yet these could hardly be thought of as hindering the SVTC programme. In fact, these are suggestive of enormous potential and capacities. Similar is the case with the location of the residence of the trainees: Most of the trainees are from adjoining neighbourhoods and they adhere to the SVTC time-schedule without hitch or hesitation. Is SVTC able to exploit these facilitating conditions to its advantage?

4

CAPACITY BUILDING

FOR SEVERAL socio-cultural reasons, many population groups in the country have not kept pace with change and development. This is fully exemplified by the situation of scheduled castes. Not only have the social norms and practices discouraged them, but they themselves have been given to inertia. Perhaps 'labelling effect' has taken its toll. Taking it as their *karma,* they have reconciled with their occupying the lower rung of the socio-economic ladder. Perhaps this flows from the system–caste is people, thinking and interacting in characteristic ways (see Khan, 1995). In the post-Independence period, policies and programmes have been initiated to bring about rapid and substantive change in the situation of scheduled castes. Have we been able to evolve viable and effective intervention strategies?

No. denying the fact that an individual's capacity to perform and excel has something to do with what he inherits from his forebears. But this cannot be taken to be the sole determinant. Environment and his early experiences have a crucial role in this. Should the individual have to himself a conducive environment and enriching experience, his personality including his capacities are bound to develop. This is what SVTC aspires to accomplish.

The kind of ambience and experience SVTC provides to youngsters from Valmiki families are very much in consonance with the contemporary socio-political thinking. In post-Independence period, change and development have been a distinctive feature of the national life. Multi-pronged efforts have been made for the welfare and development of scheduled castes. These could directly be traced to several constitutional provisions. Articles 14, 15, and 16 grant all including scheduled castes unrestrained equality in all walks of life. Article 338 calls upon the state to have a mechanism to safeguard their interest (see also Chalam, 1990; Chauhan, 1990). Likewise, articles 332 and 334 provide for reservation in legislatures, educational institutions and employment. Since the very beginning, planned socio-economic development has laid emphasis on the development of these depressed classes. They are to receive priority in all rural development and poverty alleviation programmes. For example, thirty per cent of the beneficiaries of Integrated Rural Development Programme are to be from scheduled castes. Some population-specific schemes have also been introduced (for example, Indira Awas Yojana).

Beginning with the Seventh Plan, under Special Component Plan, funds have been earmarked for their development. To illustrate, under the Eighth Plan, an outlay of Rs. 2548 crores was made; and, aditionally, states were to make an allocation of Rs. 3086 crores for this purpose. Besides, there are functioning National Scheduled Castes Development Corporation and State Scheduled Castes Finance and Development Corporation.

A pointed emphasis is laid on educational and skill development among scheduled castes. Apart from reservation of seats in educational institutions, scheduled caste children are provided incentives in cash and kind. For their benefit, a chain of 'coaching' centres functions--to prepare them for admission to technical courses and for competitive examinations for jobs. Put together, does it all measure up to the problem?

The process of socio-economic liberalisation that set in early nineties has given an impetus to efforts directed at the development of scheduled castes. The continuum of education, skill development, production and export has come to occupy the centre-stage. Economic statistics, too, reflect some gains in these sectors. The gut issue however is: As to what extent have these waves of change touched underprivileged caste groups including Valmikis?

Doubtless, the backlog is enormous. It would be unfounded optimism to expect any single policy or programme to make a dent into the problem. What is called for is that well-meaning citizens, private voluntary agencies and public organisations--all join hand and mind to contribute their mite to bring the underprivileged into the mainstream of national life. This is where the SVTC assumes a pointed significance.

Seen from a larger perspective, SVTC essentially aims to build capacities of young boys and girls from Valmiki families. It helps them to become better and more self-reliant citizens, so that they lead a life of dignity. This goal would be realised to the extent SVTC is able to motivate these youngsters and impart income-generation skills. Has it been able to do this? The present section is an attempt to answer this question.

Information about SVTC

In relation to socio-economic programmes being pursued on some scale in the country, inadequacy of information, education and communication (IEC) is a major problem: Services are organized and made available, yet they are seldom optimally or purposefully utilised, mainly because the targeted are not aware or properly informed about them. The development experience brings out that many change strategies and development programmes have produced but indifferent impact, as the targeted were unaware about them or were inadequately informed. That is why, IEC is currently thought of as an integral part of development process. This is not without justification. It sensitizes people about the problem, motivates them to participate in development programmes and endows the programme with sustainability. This in view, it is important that SVTC and its activities are known to those for whom these have been designed.

TABLE 4.1: Sources of Information on SVTC

(in Percentage)

Information source	Informant	
	Trainees (N = 45)	Ex-trainees (N = 15)
Ex-trainees	53	34
Community leaders	16	20
Sulabh workers	13	20
Self-exploration	9	13
Others	9	13

It is, therefore, relevant to find out the source from which the trainees and ex-trainees first came to know about SVTC. Table 4.1 brings out relevant details. It is observed that ex-trainees have been SVTC's biggest communicators. Fifty-three per cent trainees and 34 per cent ex-trainees report that they had received information about SVTC from former trainees. Also, it very well fits into logic: When trainees spend their time at the SVTC purposefully and gainfully, and when they step out duly counselled and equipped for shouldering life-responsibilities, they become a source of authentic and convincing information to other Valmiki youngsters.

In this, Sulabh workers figure somewhat indifferently: only 13 per cent of the trainees and 20 per cent ex-trainees mention them in this regard. This hardly provides any room for complacency on the part of SVTC workers. They need to do their bit to disseminate information about SVTC. Has this been the case? The data hardly encourage this assertion. Perhaps, the outreach of SVTC would do with a second look. Sulabh International Centre for Action Sociology and SVTC workers would do well to visit communities and families, more frequently than has been hitherto possible, to spread the Sulabh message and make people aware of SVTC activities.

This apart, attempt has been made as to when trainees have first visited SVTC. It is discouraging to note that all the ex-trainees and 82 per cent trainees visited SVTC only when they had enrolled themselves for training. Perhaps SVTC may formulate and initiate more grass-roots level communication programmes. Among others, it is likely to go a long way in attracting a larger number of talented youngsters and, thereby to afford the SVTC a chance to pick up trainees having larger potential and promise.

Selection of Vocational Trade

As pointed out, SVTC offers a range of vocational training programmes. Youngsters, both Valmikis and non-Valmikis, enroll themselves in the programme in accordance with their aptitude and background (see also Thiagarajah, 1986). Nonetheless, their choice is invariably influenced by market-forces. In other words, the choice of trade is determined by goal-orientation of the youngsters. Should they feel that a particular trade has larger post-training prospects, they may opt for it, regardless of their background.

This is what comes out loud and clear when the view of trainees as well as of ex-trainees is ascertained. Three-fourths of trainees and ex-trainees give reason for selecting a particular trade at the SVTC as their desire 'to become economically independent'. Only 24 per cent of trainees mention 'general interest'. A few appear to have been attracted by the consideration of getting an ITI certificate which would subsequently help them in landing a suitable job. Also a fifth of the ex-trainees mention 'seat availability' as a reason for their choice or decision. May it be noted that, earlier on, the range of vocational trades offered by SVTC was still more limited. "I was interested in Typing trade", reported one trainee, "which had no seat available. So I thought Electrical trade will be all right." One girl-trainee in Tailoring provided a different insight, "My mother tells me that girls should be proficient in cutting and stitching so that after marriage they are more acceptable by their in-laws." However, another girl-trainee was more perceptive and radical: "In modern times, girls must engage in paid work to have position in family and community. For me, this training is a means to achieve this goal." One ex-trainee seemed to have parents deciding most of the things on his behalf: "My parents were keen that I must undergo a Sulabh Programme, whether this programme or any other".

It follows that the reasons given by trainees for selecting a given trade for training do not make for rational choices. Most of these reflect parental influence in decision-making. The possibility of this telling upon their motivational level adversely cannot be ruled out.

Skill Upgradation

All institutions emphasize on incremental learning. This has a pointed relevance to training organizations. Towards this, syllabi, sometimes with time-allocation, are prescribed. The SVTC also has this format. Indeed, several factors contribute to learning upgradation including aptitude, background and motivation of the trainees, on the one hand, and institutional infrastructure, on the other. The SVTC has a system of proper evaluation or examination at the end of the course. While trainees in Electrical, Tailoring and Typing are examined by ITI professionals, those in other trades by SVTC staff. Not all trainees are able to make the grade. In part, this could be traced to the nature of clientele the SVTC is called upon to serve: Coming from weaker sections of society, not all the trainees have requisite background or aptitude. Nonetheless, trainees who are unable to make the grade in these examinations, are awarded certificate by the SVTC that they attended 'Hobby Course''.

At the same time, relevant in this regard is the subjective perception of the trainees. In this, the time-period a trainee has been in the programme is considerably important. Stated differently, those trainees who have been pursuing a programme longer would ordinarily find themselves ahead on the uptake--as compared with those who have been on the programme for a shorter period.

Towards this, the opinion of SVTC instructors has been ascertained. Most of them (86 per cent) think that Valmikis are interested in learning the trade; and all of them think that Valmiki trainees are as quick on the uptake as non-Valmiki trainees are. There are however a few dissenting voices too: ''Most of the trainees particularly Valmiki trainees, are engaged in one job or the other on the side'', remarked one instructor, ''how could they concentrate on the training programme, as this would amount to losing income howsoever small?"

Equally important in this regard is the viewpoint of the trainees. It is found (see Table 4.2) that only a third of the SVTC trainees state that they have learnt much and the remaining state that they have learnt something or a few things. Does the opinion of the trainees differ with the amount of time they have spent on the programme?

TABLE 4.2: Training duration and reported learning upgradation

Months	Learning Upgradation		Total
	Learnt something	Learnt much	
Less than one	1	--	1
One to two	9	7	16
Two or more	17	11	28
Total	27	18	45

A reference to Table 4.2 would show that 40 per cent of the trainees who have been undergoing training for one to two months state that they have learnt much. This proportion falls to 39 per cent in respect of those who have been on the training programme for two months or more. Most of these trainees belong either to Driving trade (total training duration, 3 months) or Typing trade (duration, 6 months).

Taken together, the viewpoint of the trainees is hardly encouraging. Although these are subjective perceptions, these may have a bearing on the effectiveness of the programme and may have some correlation with the ultimate outcome. Given this, Training methodology calls for a review and streamlining.

To recapitulate, SVTC symbolises an ambitious enterprize which aims to enter into the life of Valmiki youngsters. It offers structured programmes directed at their skill upgradation. How do the youngsters respond to this?

SVTC communication inputs would do well to further enlarge and intensify so that Valmiki youngsters are a little more aware of it and its diverse activities. It may increase the possibility of trainees identifying themselves with Sulabh Movement, its goal and SVTC work. Furthermore, such communication inputs may attract a larger number of talented youngsters who would opt to train in a particular trade as their conscious choice. It is they who are likely to move faster towards skill upgradation. Perhaps this perspective would become clearer when we look into the impact of SVTC programmes.

5

PROGRAMME OUTCOMES

DOUBTLESS, SVTC's programmes are ambitious. These have a three-fold inter-connected purposes: weaning away Valmiki youngsters from their traditional vocations, providing them with a viable alternative and socially rehabilitating them in community and society. It follows that the primary focus of SVTC is on skill-development from which everything else flows. Having attained a certain level of proficiency in a given trade, Valmiki youngsters are likely to become economically self-reliant and psychologically self-confident. In turn, their status in community and society is likely to go up.

The above in view, the present discussion takes a closer look at the social environment in the SVTC and post-training work and position of trainees in the community.

SOCIAL ENVIRONMENT IN THE SVTC

Apart from instruction and skill development, informal interaction between Valmiki trainees and other around them forcefully defines the social environment of the SVTC and its role in the fulfilment of explicit or implicit objectives. This is critically important to influence antiquated norms and practices of the caste system which is as much a pattern of highly differentiated relationships as it is a state of mind.

Assuredly, Sulabh Movement impliedly intends to modify it so as to make it a little more just and equitable. Has such a conducive environment been available to Valmiki youngsters on the SVTC campus?

Peer Group

Sharing of such an activity as SVTC programmes provides trainees a basis to develop a bond of mutual understanding and just friendship. Does it happen? In the opinion of all the instructors, trainees befriend with each other regardless of their castes. The ground reality does not however fully support this contention.

TABLE 5.1: Closest friend of Valmiki-trainees

(in Percentage)

Friend	Caste	Respondent	
		Trainee	Ex-trainee
First closest	Valmiki	56	64
	Non-Valmiki	44	36
Second closest	Valmiki	52	50
	Non-Valmiki	48	50
Third closest	Valmiki	59	46
	Non-Valmiki	41	54

The friend circle of Valmiki trainees is characterised by a preponderance of Valmiki youngsters (see Table 5.1). It is found that 56 per cent of Valmiki trainees have a Valmiki as their first closest friend. The trend persists in respect of second closest (52 per cent) and third closest (59 per cent) friend. Nevertheless, it is gratifying that Valmiki trainees have a substantial proportion of non-Valmiki friends.

A stronger trend is discerned, in respect of ex-trainees. As reported by them, their first closest friend is a Valmiki (64 per cent). However the proportion of non-Valmiki friends increases when their second closest (50 per cent) and third closest (54 per cent) friends are considered. This kind of composition of peer group may have something to do with the location (Delhi is a metropolitan city), yet the enabling role of the SVTC, to a great extent, is in evidence.

Social Visits

Yet another form of interaction is visit to the residence of friends. Still more important in the present context are return visits. While these do indicate affiliation and social intermixing, these also depend upon the population mix of neighbourhoods and available means of transport. This apart, visits lower caste segregation and discrimination, and reduce linear distance (see Bogardus, 1960). It is observed that a third of the trainees have visited the residences of their non-Valmiki course-mates (see Table 5.2). Most of them have done it recently, within the preceding month. The situation of ex-trainees is distinctly more positive: Four-fifths of them have done so, and three-fourths among them have done so during preceding one month.

TABLE 5.2: Social house-visits exchanged by trainees.

	Percentages
R visiting non-Valmiki course-mates	
Trainees	33
Ex-trainees	80
Non-Valmiki course-mates visiting R	
Trainees	40
Ex-trainees	73

R = Respondent

How about return visits? Visits of non-Valmiki trainees to the residence of Valmiki course-mates are however fewer: only two-fifths of the Valmiki trainees report such visits by their non-Valmiki course-mates (Table 5.2). These visits have come about only recently. However, the trend is more substantial in respect of ex-trainees. More than 73 per cent of the ex-trainees report visit of their non-Valmiki course-mates to their residence, and 82 per cent of these visits have been during the preceding month. Seemingly, Valmiki trainees are somewhat inhibited in their interaction or adjustment with their non-Valmiki course-mates. Like their predecessors, with the passage of time, they may not remain so. The homogenising influence of a metropolis notwithstanding, SVTC and its programmes appear to promote and enlarge this kind of interaction and *bon ami.*

Inter-dining

Indeed, SVTC endeavours to mitigate caste differences. Even otherwise, modern industrial organisations hardly brook denominational considerations. Ordinarily, it could be presumed that industrial culture including vocational training would suppress caste norms and practices and would emphasise on performance and team work. To what extent caste stereo-types are suppressed is reflected by such day-to-day behaviour as peer group interaction in training institutions. In this inter-dining stands out (Anant, 1975).

Sharing of food has a significant place in caste norms. Does SVTC soften the conformity to these norms by the trainees? It needs to be pointed out that vocational training programmes run by the SVTC do not have a uniform time-schedule. All the five programmes run in two shifts, that is, morning and evening. As a result, few trainees bring their tiffin. But there are several Sulabh functions, during which trainees eat snacks or full meals together. Do they share or exchange food items?

The opinion of a majority of instructors (86 per cent) is in the negative. This is somewhat understandable: They do not share food as few trainees bring lunch; and during functions sharing of food is just not required. So is the opinion of two-thirds of ex-trainees (at the work-place, sharing food with co-workers) and 84 per cent of the trainees. It may well be noted that attitude towards inter-dining is more important than sharing of food itself. In this regard, quite a few trainees are found favourably predisposed towards inter-dining. Thirty-three per cent of the ex-trainees and 15 per cent of the trainees report two-way sharing of the food with co-workers or course-mates. Among other things, this ground reality forcefully underlines the tenacity and persistence of caste norms governing food or commensalism.

Class-Room Ambience

Reinforcement of caste norms also takes place in instructional setting--through mostly minor and seemingly insignificant interaction. Participation of students or trainees in the upkeep of the classroom is hardly exceptionable; but it does become exceptionable if a particular group is asked to do this all too often. The same goes with seating arrangement: Who regularly occupies back benches? Yet another issue is the enforcement of discipline; Is any particular group subject to relatively vigorous discipline? These and similar issues assume considerable significance in relation to the SVTC, as four out of five Hindu instructors belong to upper castes and the possibility of subtle discrimination is not easy to rule out (Gill, 1989).

In the opinion of the instructors, Valmiki trainees are as much responsive to instructions as non-Valmiki trainees. Similar is the matter with discipline. This is also borne out by attendance, evaluation and occasional awards to trainees. A minor exception to this is Electrical trade. As most of the trainees in this trade reportedly engage in sundry job or work, they do not pay due attention to punctuality, regularity and instruction.

What is the trainee-perspective? All the trainees and also ex-trainees report that instructors do not insist on any particular seating arrangement (for example, Valmiki students being assigned to back-benches). Similar is the matter with the upkeep of the classroom: The SVTC has regular arrangement for sweeping and mopping and for tidying up of the rooms. Occasionally students also dust doors and furnitures. But it is done by all the trainees regardless of their lineage or caste.

Similarly, all the trainees and ex-trainees report enforcement of discipline being equitable. If ever any instructor raises a finger or voice, it is because of the situation and behaviour of the trainee rather than his background. Data are thus convergent that at the SVTC the instructor-trainee interaction is almost totally free from caste-bias. Perhaps much of this springs from Sulabh ideology and thrust.

POST-TRAINING WORK

Occupational aspirations are critical in one's life scheme (Deb and Aggarwal, 1974). These may be thought of as orientation towards occupational goals (Heller and Miller, 1963) which operate within two bounds called idealistic and realistic. The level of idealistic occupational aspiration is an individual's preference for the occupation which he intends to enter into. On the other hand, the level of realistic occupational aspiration is the lowest expectation of an individual considering his ways and means and the natural and social barriers. In traditional Hindu society, caste system and occupations used to be inter-linked. The occupation to be followed by an individual when of age would be determined by the caste in which he was born. This is what SVTC intends to break. Has it been able to move in this direction?

Before we look into the work which Valmiki youngsters have undertaken after having been through the SVTC, we need to take stock of the occupational aspirations of the trainees. Indeed, these aspirations vary with vocational trades. To illustrate, trainees in Beauty-care expect to get a job in a beauty-parlour, and a few to set up their own parlour. These in Driving trade hope to get a job in a private or government organization (one trainee aspires for Army). Those in Electrical trade have a larger range of choices: self-employment, salaried job, business, etc. "First I would look for service", chuckled a trainee doing Electrical trade, "if I do not manage to do so, *apna haath Jagannath,* I will set up may own business." So is however not the case with those in Tailoring: They hoped to work at home, tailoring-shop or garment-factory. Some of them cherished hopes to set up their own business, even of garment export. One exuberant girl-trainee was in high spirits, "After completing my training in Tailoring, I'll set up a training centre in my neighbourhood and make many more girls skilled and self-reliant.'' Most ambitious are however those in Typing trade. Of course, they think of a salaried job but the range is wide--from clerk-typist to civil services. Interestingly, a few of them are crazy about government job: ''I have to have a government job, may it be even that of a sweeper.'' Another young person was less hopeful, ''These days, you require influence or money to get a job. I have neither.'' More often than not, expectations of parents or husbands, as reported by trainees, run parallel to that of their own. The issue is whether SVTC programmes bring these dreams closer to fulfilment.

Are instructional programmes of the SVTC *market-relevant?* Again, on this, opinion of ex-trainees differs from trade to trade. It may well be kept in mind that ex-trainees whose opinion has been ascertained have undergone training only in Electrical, Tailoring and Typing trades. While those who have spent time on Tailoring and Typing are almost unanimous that the trades are subsequently useful for having meaningful, satisfying and remunerative work. Those in Electrical trade are somewhat divided on the issue. Their major disagreement is on the duration of training: It is of six months only, whereas most prospective employers look for ITI pattern which is spread over 12 to 24 months. On the whole, SVTC. skill-development programmes generally manage to prepare young people for remunerative job or work.

All things considered, the main issue is of trainees securing proper work, once they have successfully completed their training programme. This apart, there are certain limiting conditions, for example, job-market being tight or trainees still pursuing higher education (there are in the SVTC such eight trainees). Reportedly, in many organizations, prospective employers are obliged to make under-hand payment for securing a job--temporary or regular. Yet another

TABLE 5.3: Perceived difficulty in securing job/work after training at the SVTC.

(in Percentage)

Respondents	Response	
	No	Yes
Instructors (N = 7)	71	29
Trainees (N = 36)	75	25
Ex-Trainees (N = 13)	92	8

limiting condition could be covert caste discriminating on the part of the employers.

What is the contemporary scenario like? A reference to Table 5.3 would show that a large proportion of instructors (29 per cent) apprehend that ex-trainees would or do face difficulty in securing a job or work. This proportion is lower in the estimation of current trainees (25 per cent). That it is still lower in respect of ex-trainees (8 per cent) is highly significant and encouraging. These perceptions do hint at three positive possibilities: (1) SVTC training is goal-oriented and effective, (2) work environment in Delhi is liberal and progressive, and (3) caste restrictions are steadily going down.

Next, attention may be diverted to the *placement* of trainees passing out from SVTC. Four-fifths of the ex-trainees are found to be engaged in meaningful and remunerative work. Still more notable is the fact that none of them is engaged in hereditary or traditional work (namely, scavenging). Should such a trend endure, it is bound to herald far-reaching structural changes.

How much income do the ex-trainees raise? Such a consideration a highly relevant to the issues under discussion. Among others, it is likely to provide an assessment as to what extent deflection of Valmikis from traditional occupations has been a change for the better. At the same time, it may well be kept in mind that the income of the ex-trainees depends on the trade they have been trained in.

For example, Tailoring trainees, most of them women and girls, work from home on job-basis. Some of them earn as little as Rs. 200 a month. On the other hand, those who were trained in the Electrical trade are certainly better off. Some of them are engaged in salaried jobs and also handle private work on the side--making as much as Rs. 2500 a month. On an average, these young persons, in their new pursuit, are able to generate Rs. 1125 a month. Taken together, the situation seems to be quite encouraging. The SVTC programme does manage to give a break to Valmiki youngsters.

POSITION IN SOCIETY

Work, honest to goodness work, has definite bearing on the social position one has in family, community and society. In other words, performance and excellence in work go a long way in elevating one's social status. These precepts are equally valid for the Valmiki youngsters. What is the ground situation?

In this connection, this issue has been brought up with ex-trainees and their opinion has been ascertained about their position in the peer group and community during and after the training at SVTC. Nearly three-fourths of them have indicated their views. All of them feel that after training at the SVTC, boys and girls of their age-group have started listening to them more seriously. This is also the case, as reported by four-fifths of the ex-trainees, with the community: Elderly people in the neighbourhood listen to them and pay more attention. Even otherwise, it is a common observation that people and society respect those who perform and achieve. SVTC trainees are no exception to this. In a way, this paves the way for the emergence of a new 'Little Tradition'. Furthermore, should this come about on a larger scale, caste barriers are bound to go down.

It would be thus seen that Sulabh and the SVTC are slowly but steadily moving towards their avowed goal, namely, weaning Valmiki youngsters from their demeaning ancestral occupations and diverting them to modern pursuits. What is more notable is the fact that, in this process, they are also promoting egalitarianism in society.

6

CONCLUSION

NOTIONS of purity and pollution inherent in the caste system have characterised social milieu in India--for millennia. It would not take long to see that these notions militate with the aspirations of a democratic and progressive nation. That a whole pupulation group is relegated to unclean or socially degrading work, generation after generation, is neither just nor equitable. What is more, such antiquated predispositions towards institutionalised inequities have hampered the task of nation-building in no small way.

Much of this could be traced to hoary caste traditions based on *varna*. Maybe, in the beginning, *varna* system was based on *guna* and *karma*. Maybe it was some kind of division of work. And, maybe, it was functional. But, in distant past, its basis shifted from *karma* to *janama,* and caste started being determined by his or her birth. As is well known, caste is structure with well-defined status, roles and modes of inter-group relations. Who would do what when of age, all is predetermined. In this social equation, Sudras particularly Valmikis, have been at the receiving end.

Doubtless, institutionalised inequities were over-stretched when entire caste groups were labelled as unapproachable or untouchable. What is more, although Valmikis were assigned essential functions of hygiene and sanitation (scavenging, midwifery, removing and flaying of dead animals, etc.), they were considered socially impure and untouchable. This also resulted in numerous civil disabilities. Society created and imposed this kind of hierarchical social order to the disadvantage of Sudras or Valmikis. However, ironically enough, they also accepted it. Probably, Sudras were comparatively less informed, educated and skilled, and therefore were not in a position to articulate philosophies to their advantage. On the other hand, they imbibed philosophies of *karma* and *punar janama.* These explained their lowly position in society and compelled them to reconcile with their plight. Also these promised them improvement in their social status in subsequent births, should they conduct themselves in accordance with caste norms. The possibility is strong that Sudras, more or less, accepted the label. Over the centuries, they appear to have been given to inertia or even stoicism.

Indeed, in time and space, such institutionalised inequities have not gone unnoticed. From time to time, it did engage the attention of powers that be. However, seldom has this gone beyond lip-service. In the post-Independence era, the problem of untouchability as well as pervasive socio-economic backwardness received a pointed attention of policy-makers. Untouchability was legally abolished and a plethora of policies and programmes were initiated for the upliftment of scheduled castes. Ever since, endeavour in this direction has never ceased or slowed. In this, social intervention and educational programmes have occupied centre-stage and rightly so. Should members of scheduled castes surge forward in education and skill-development, they would be able to avoid those pitfalls which they have had in ancient and medieval times.

Towards this, seats are reserved in educational institutions, scheduled castes students are exempt from payment of fees and, in many states, they are provided incentives in cash and kind. Somehow, their proportion in literacy and education in not growing the way it should have, and it is found to be far below the national average.

On the other hand, boys and girls from scheduled caste households are yet to take to skill-development in a substantial way. This could be attributed to two main factors: During vocational training they have to forgo, partially or fully, daily-wages; and most of them aspire for government job (be it only in Group D). At the same time, skill-development is so many things in one, especially for those who have not done much schooling. With the process of socio-economic liberalisation introduced in early nineties, skill-development offers much promise and wide scope.

Against this backdrop, the work being done by Sulabh International Social Service Organisation (SISSO) stands out. It has taken the problem of untouchability head on. It made the concept of low-cost sanitation a reality in the four quarters of the country. What is more, it provided a range of educational and skill-development alternatives to youngsters from Valmiki households--so that they move up in education and skill-development, acquire self-esteem and self-reliance and achieve harmonious social adjustment or readjustment. Sulabh Vocational Training Centre (SVTC) is a logical corollary to this larger approach.

Set up in 1992, it has two main objectives: (a) Skill-development, and (b) social adjustment. Put together, these are likely to pave the way for a substantial and enduring socio-economic reintegration of Valmiki youngsters into society. It is in keeping with the approach of Sulabh Movement: Attack the cause and heal the effect. SVTC approach is evolutionary in thrust. It heads for gradual but enduring change in social structure. Nonetheless, the gut issue is: To what extent has the SVTC been able to achieve this goal?

The present work is meant to take an incisive look into the organisation and functioning of the SVTC, to assess the level of involvement of all concerned, and to ascertain the extent of socio-economic reintegration Valmiki boys and girls are able to have. Towards this, a substantial number of instructors, employers, trainees and ex-trainees have been interacted with. Preceding account presents relevant information, their analysis and interpretation. What is the picture that emerges from these diverse sources of information?

Skill Development

It may be reiterated that SVTC goes beyond pious pronouncements and adopts a pragmatic approach for diverting Valmiki boys and girls from their traditional occupations. It heads for skill upgradation in five vocational trades, namely Beauty-care, Driving, Electrical, Tailoring and Typing. By doing so, it expects them to embark upon a path of self-esteem and self-reliance. Does it have appropriate support structures to achieve these goals?

The SVTC has a small but effective organisational set-up (see Fig. 2.1). The responsibility of day-to-day supervision and coordination is shouldered by Vice-Chairman-cum-Director. Thus far, SVTC's financial accounting procedures have been more informal than being systematic. The main source of funding has been SISSO. In this regard, some budgetary procedures are also adopted. Till now, it has also worked. That SVTC considers undertaking regularly budgetary exercise is not without merit. Budget is not only a statement of income and expenditure but also a method of organisational planning--so crucial for sustained and balanced growth.

The SVTC is relatively well off in terms of physical facilities. Every trade has a room to itself, size of the room varying in accordance with the requirements of the trade. However, in the opinion of instructors, Beauty-care and

Electrical trades would do with some more space. All the five trades are provided with necessary equipments. Nevertheless, there is always room for improvement. For instance, Beauty-care would do with one or two additional stuffed chairs; Driving with a few more training vehicles (for example, Padmini, Ambassador, truck, etc.); Electrical with tool-kits; Tailoring with electric-powered sewing machines and embroidery and pekoe on machines; Typing with electronic type-writer and computer. Maybe these requirements are taken up in a phased manner.

It is gratifying to note that the SVTC has a band of committed, qualified and competent instructors. Typically, an instructor is a caste Hindu, male and aged 28 years. Possibly he commutes to Mahavir Enclave seven kilometres a day. On the average, he has a monthly income of Rs.2,040. That he is generally fair-minded and interested in trainees' skill development is borne by the view of the trainees.

Indeed, stipend is contentious issue about which trainees as well as instructors have divergent opinions. At any rate, particularly for Valmiki boys and girls, stipend is a big attraction. Many organisations engaged in similar activities offer this to them--mostly with public support of funding. Therc seems to be a strong case that the SVTC resumes giving stipend to Valmiki trainees, maybe on a truncated scale, and may be on merit-cum-attendance basis. Towards this, the Ministry of Welfare could also be approached.

Except for driving, remaining four trades have regular syllabi which are handed down both to instructors and trainees. These largely conform to those in use with ITIs. Nevertheless, these syllabi could be further enriched to keep pace with changing market demands.

At the same time, SVTC is fortunate to have boys and girls of potential and capability. Out of every five trainees, two are from Valmiki families. SVTC does have 'preference' for them, yet like everybody else they undergo prescribed admission procedure. A typical trainee (both Valmiki and non-Valmiki trainees included) is unmarried, aged 20 and has been to school. Every day the trainee travels a distance of about four kilometres to participate in the training programme. Not very clear about the choice of the trade, the trainee aspires to have a break in life--maybe some day his aspirations turn into reality.

Certainly SVTC programmes lead to skill upgradation. In this regard, the views of trainees, ex-trainees and instructors are unanimous. This is further supported by the evaluation of examination conducted on the completion of training programmes. It is notable that examination in most of the trades are conducted by ITI personnel; and it is ITI which awards certificate to successful trainees.

The assertion of skill development is also reinforced by *placement* of the boys and girls passing out from the SVTC. Many of them engage in salaried jobs, some take to self-employment and a few start their own business. It is remarkable that quite a few trainees are ambitious and dream of doing well in life. In any case, those who had passed out in previous years are engaged in economically gainful work making as much as Rs. 2,500 a month.

Environmental Awareness

The axiom 'Information is strength' is found to be specially valid in contemporary times. As mentioned, in post-Independence period, numerous policies and programmes have been initiated for the upliftment of weaker sections of society, particularly Valmikis. However, results of these have hardly been commensurate to efforts. Stated differently, Valmikis have not benefited from these to the extent they should have. This could largely be traced to low environmental awareness on the part of Valmikis themselves.

Caste norms and practices have instilled inertia in

Valmikis. Most of them are given even to stoicism. Despite radical changes in the socio-political environment, they have low self-esteem and sense of efficacy. Little do they see what future has in store for them.

What is more, Valmikis especially those in rural and slum areas have low access to information about the programmes in progress for their upliftment. While most development programmes have a built-in component of information, education and communication, proper and sufficient information rarely percolates to the grass-roots level. As a result, their felt and unfelt needs are seldom met adequately.

Yet another consideration is of motivation--motivation to change and to experience growth. In fact, this has something to do with the inertia hammered into them for centuries. On the other hand, few change agents, most of them government functionaries, make any conscious effort to pull them out from inertia and put them on the road to dignity, prosperity and happiness. Are voluntary agencies doing something in this area of vital concern?

In this regard, SVTC is well-placed. Located in the capital city, it has Valmiki boys and girls who are exposed to a diverse range of media of mass communication. City-life has perpetual avalanche of information put out by print, electronic and other media. Directly or indirectly, these have levelling effect. To a good deal, it may have a salutary effect on caste differences and cleavages. Secondly, it has something to do with expectations in life, particularly of those tender in age. In all likelihood, it may have something to do with their aspirations and life-goals.

Nonetheless, it is observed, at the SVTC information dissemination and environmental awareness have not received thus far the kind of priority these deserve. In fact, few systematic attempts have been made to reach the message of Sulabh Movement to scheduled castes or Valmikis at the grass-roots level. Prior to enrolling in the vocational trade, very few trainees had any substantial information about Sulabh Movement or SVTC.

The role of SVTC in promoting development awareness is at best indirect. During the course of interaction with instructors or class-mates, trainees pick up tidbits on development programmes. As at present, few direct or deliberate efforts are made to expose them to development programmes, the opportunities these offer and the procedures to be completed to avail of them. Assuredly, something substantial needs to be done in this area.

Social Adjustment

The SVTC and its activities are by no means concerned only with skill upgradation among boys and girls from Valmiki households. These have a larger social purpose behind them, namely, social reintegration of Valmikis. At the same time, their problems are linked with certain larger issues. Over the centuries, caste-system has spawned and strengthened institutionalised inequities which, in turn, have given rise to civil disabilities and differential economic opportunities. To a good deal, the two overlap. While civil disabilities have, to a great extent, been taken care of through legal means, the task of balancing the unjust economic order remains largely unfinished. The SVTC addresses itself to this task. In other words, through skill upgradation it aims to bring about a better and enduring social adjustment between Valmikis and social environment.

As a matter of fact, redoubled efforts need to be made to promote education and skill among scheduled castes, particularly among Valmikis. It is through these that they can establish harmonious relations with physical and social environment, and surmount social barriers erected by the caste system. Given this, SVTC activities tend to become a psycho-physical strategy to pull them out of age-old inertia and integrate them into the national mainstream. Has this been possible to bring about?

Indeed, the SVTC has been able to cover some distance in this direction. This is borne out by the situation obtaining on and off the SVTC campus. In the class-room, Valmiki trainees sit with others without any consideration of their background. Instructors maintain parity in their dealing. Given the situation, Valmiki trainees share food with their non-Valmiki course-mates. They and their predecessors whole-heartedly participate in SVTC and Sulabh functions. Yet their peer group comprises mostly Valmiki youngsters.

The situation obtaining off the SVTC campus is somewhat unclear. Off and on, trainees do pay a home-visit to their non-Valmikis course-mates. However, return visits are fewer. Adjustment at the workplace had little that would be exceptionable. Reportedly, ex-trainees along with their non-Valmiki co-workers sit down at their workplace to have lunch together. Should a situation arise, they also exchange food. Having undergone skill development and taken up proper job, they receive more attention in their neighbourhood.

All things considered, SVTC activities make for an important mechanism to promote social adjustment. Thus far, it has been largely an unintended outcome. Perhaps, modalities could be evolved to speed up the process consciously and substantially.

Goal Fulfilment

The SVTC has adopted an innovative approach to mitigate the problem of caste inequality and put the disadvantaged on the path of self-esteem and dignity. It has many accomplishments to its credit. In the class-room, the quality of instruction is acceptable, if not high. This is also shown

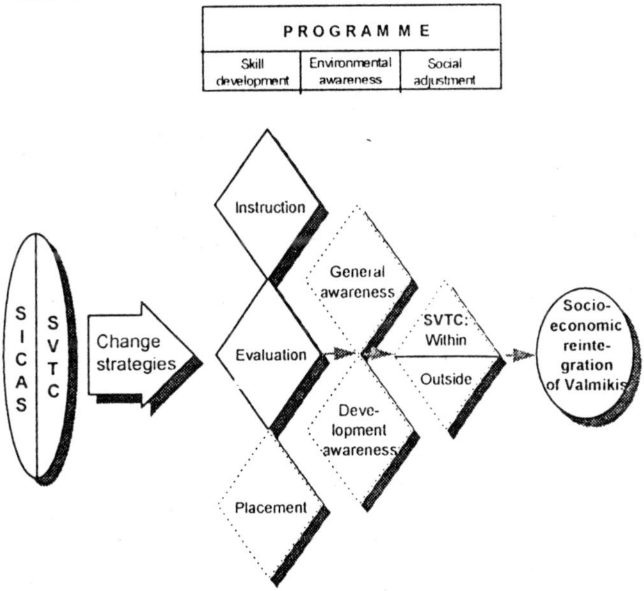

FIG. 6.1: Social intervention strategy of SVTC

by the evaluations, in most cases, conducted by outside specialists. Its alumni, albeit limited in number, are doing rather well in life. Indeed, these are some of the more visible and verifiable outcomes.

On the other hand, some headway has been made in promoting environmental awareness, social adjustment and social reintegration among Valmiki trainees. This encourages hope that, in the years to come, they would be as much participatory citizens as persons of self-esteem and dignity.

This is not to say that little could be done to widen the scope of SVTC and to strengthen its activities. Figure 6.1 presents the overall perspective the SVTC has or should have. Moving towards the goal of socio-economic reintegration of Valmikis, it is actualising change strategies by initiating a programme of activities including skill-development, environmental awareness and social adjustment. In this, it has been more effective in imparting instruction, evaluation and certification. But, in the matter of placement of trainees, it has been less than effective. So is the matter with environmental awareness and social adjustment.

By way of further improvement, the SVTC would do well to pay attention and prioritise certain emergent issues. Modalities could be evolved to reach out the message of Sulabh Movement to a wider audience, at least throughout the NCT of Delhi, prticularly at the neighbourhood level, Along with this, boys and girls from Valmiki households could be informed about the SVTC activities. Secondly, trades like Beauty-care, Driving, Electrical, Tailoring and Typing would do well with some updating. Thirdly, a few more market-relevant trades could be added. Fourthly, a pointed attention could be paid to liaison with prospective employers towards having proper placement of those successfully completing various training programmes. Fifthly, trainees in different trades could be exposed to the range of socio-economic opportunities available to them and to the development programmes offered by government and voluntary organisations. Lastly, deliberate and systematic efforts could be made to bring about, to begin with, a harmonious social adjustment between Valmiki trainees and the social milieu.

All things considered, the SVTC confidently marches ahead in the hope that young boys and girls from Valmiki families would soon be on the road to dignity leading to a just social order.

BIBLIOGRAPHY

Aggarwal, Y. and Sibou, S. (1992): *Educating Scheduled Castes,* New Delhi: NIEPA, 1992.

Anant, S. S. (1975): The changing inter-caste attitudes in north India: A follow-up after four years, *European Journal of Social Psychology,* 197, 5 (1), pp. 49-59.

Bogardus, E. S. (1960): *Social Distance: The Development of Social Thoughts,* Bombay: Vakil, Feffer & Simons Pvt Ltd.

Chalam, K. S. (1990): Caste reservation and equality of opportunity in education, *Economic and Political Weekly,* 25, 41.

Chauhan, Devraj (1990): Educational and occupational levels of SCs and STs, *Mainstream,* 28, 42, p. 18.

Deb, P. C. and Aggrawal, B.K. (1974): Occupational aspiration and socio-cultural background of postgraduate students, *Interdiscipline,* 11 (2) pp. 113-121.

Desai, I. P. (1978): *Untouchability in Rural Gujarat,* Bombay: Popular Prakashan.

Dogra, Bharat (1990): For the benefit of the opponents of reservation, *Mainstream,* 28, 52, p. 20.

Domont, Louis (1970): *Homo Hierarchicus,* London: Wedenfield and Nicholson.

Furnivall, J. S. (1939): *Netherlands and India: A Study in Plural Economy,* Cambridge: Cambridge University Press.

Gill, M. S. and Singh, A. M. (1989): Reactionary dissent by caste Hindu employees, *Social Change,* 19, 3.

Government of India: Eighth Five-Year Plan Reports, New Delhi: Planning Commission.

Hutton, H. J. (1955): *Caste in India,* London: Oxford University Press.

Joshi, P. (1968) Caste: As it exist today, *Indian Psychological Review,* 4 (2), pp. 151-54.

Kamat, A. R. (1981): Education and social change amongst the scheduled castes and scheduled tribes, *Economic and Political Weekly,* 16 (31).

Khan, M. Z. and N. Prabha Unnithan (1991); Inter-caste conflict and violence: An empirical examination of its bases *International Journal of Group Tensions,* 21, 2.

Khan, M.Z. and Furqan Qamar (1996): *Scheduled Castes: Their Development Participation and Aspirations,* New Delhi: Inter-India Publications.

Masilamani, S. (1986): Educational achievement of a scheduled caste: Sex Bias--a case study of Chakkiliyars of Chinnathadagam village, *Social Action,* 36.

Nanduram (1988): *The Mobile Scheduled Caste: Rise of New Middle Class,* New Delhi: Hindustan Publishing Corporation.

Papola, T. S. and Ashraf, M.S. (1983): *Socio-economic Development of Scheduled Castes in Uttar Pradesh,* Lucknow: GIDS.

Pathak, Bindeshwar (1981): *Sulabh Shauchalaya,* Patna: Anmol Prakashan.

Pathak, Bindeshwar (1991): *Man and his Mission,* New Delhi: Sulabh International.

Pathak, Bindeshwar (1995): *Road to Freedom: A Sociological Study on the Abolition of Scavenging in India,* Delhi: Motilal Banarsidas Publishers Pvt Ltd.

Prakash, Nirupama (1989): *Scheduled Castes; Socio-economic Changes,* Allahabad: Chugh Publications.

Prasad, P. H. (1990): Reservation and class structure of castes, *Economic and Political Weekly,* 25, 2.

Ram, Jagjivan (1980): *Caste Challange in India,* New Delhi: Vision Books.

Rao, Mohan U.S. (Ed.) (1968): *The Message of Mahatma Gandhi,* New Delhi: Publication Division.

Rao, Bhat and Venkataramana (1989): Rural housing among scheduled castes in two districts of Andhra Pradesh--A comparison of parameters and prediction, *Social Change,* 19, 3.

Shah, Ghanshyam (1985): Caste, class and reservation, *Economic and Political Weekly,* 20, 3.

Sherring, M.A. (1974): *Hindu Castes and Tribes,* New Delhi: Cosmos.

Showeb, M. (1986): *Education and Mobility among Harijans,* Allahabad: Vohra Publishers.

Shyamlal (1984): *The Bhangis in Transition,* New Delhi: Inter-India.

Shyamlal (1992): *The Bhangi, A Sweeper Caste. Its Socio-economic Portraits.* Bombay: Popular Prakashan.

Singh, Y. (1973): *Modernization of Indian Tradition.* New Delhi; Thompson.

Thakur, D. S.; Sharma, K.C. and Kaur, Jasminder (1984): Socio-economic conditions of scavengers in Himachal Pradesh, *Social Change,* 19, 3.

Thiagarajah, A.P. (1986): Occupational preferences of scheduled caste students, *Indian Educational Review,* 21, pp. 1-4.

INDEX